Life, Love and Lilies

Everyday Spirituality

BY

Brenda Strickland

This book is dedicated to my mother, Martha Sydenstricker Bunch, who has always seen me as a whole, wise and perfect Child of God,

To the memory and legacy of my father, Dale Dillon Bunch, who embraced the metaphysical teachings of the Fillmores and shared them with me in countless profound and precious conversations, and

To my beloved husband, John Strickland, whose steadfast and unflagging love and affirmation have made this work a joyful reality.

Table of Contents

Acknowledgements

Warmest thanks to:

Rev. John Strickland, who suggested the project and supported me every step of the way;
Martha Bunch, who introduced me to Unity Sunday School when I was 2 years old and kept bringing me back;
Dorothy Lathom, the Sunday School teacher who taught me how to go into the Silence when I was ten;
Faith Hamilton-Trent, Karen Hinton, Patty O'Keefe-Hutton, Scottie O'Toole and Beverly Armento, who believe in me and cheer me on;
Dr. Robert G. Peters, who introduced me to the three big questions;
Ann Lurie Berlin, who has waited 30 years for me to finally do this, and whose wisdom and encouragement are my guide stones;
Barbara Arrington, Wayne Manning, Tricia Reed and Neal Vahle for their meticulous reading and wise suggestions;
C. J. Trent-Gurbuz, whose thorough editing and incisive comments brought greater clarity and universality;
Pam Johnson, Patsi Yarborough, Dannie Jennings, Joy Williams, Xiomara Malagon and Greer Yarborough, the dedicated staff at Atlanta Unity who shared such profound insights as we read the book together;
Jane Adamson, Connie Ahalt, Joan Atkins, Maureen Burke and Jacqui Miller, whose questions and comments created such powerful Monday evenings, and
Atlanta Unity, the rich soil in which this book took root and bore fruit.

Introduction

Life, love and lilies are such everyday ideas – beautiful and wonderful and all around us. We forget to enjoy them sometimes, but when we remember to take a look and a deep breath, the wonder sweeps through us anew. Our connection with spirit is a lot like that – we forget it exists most of the time, but when that rare moment of remembering sweeps over us, we catch our breath and shake our heads in amazement.

Everyday spirituality means living day to day, in the world, fully conscious of oneself as a spiritual being. Spiritual consciousness can take place in a blinding flash, as it did for Saul of Tarsus on the road to Damascus. He was blinded, had an auditory experience of the Divine and, after he recovered, became the Apostle Paul (Acts 9:1-20). More likely, though, you and I will awaken to spiritual consciousness one thought, one word, one act at a time.

The purpose of this book is to draw you nearer to the highest ideal you can conceive. I believe in you. I believe that you are a divine idea in the mind of God. I believe in the vital importance of you as an integral component of the Universe. You are here now so that you can make your contribution to the welfare of us all.

The butterfly effect is the popular name for a mathematical model used in meteorology. The basic idea is that the movement of the wings of one butterfly affects the formation of a hurricane in another part of the planet. Just imagine the impact of your daily activity on the physical, emotional, mental and spiritual climates of those in your immediate environment.

Beloved, you are the embodiment of a divine idea. Rest in the knowledge that you are created to love, to bless, to create and to be happy. May this book support you in opening the doors to your future and soaring into your best life imaginable!

Brenda Strickland
Atlanta, GA
Fourth printing, March, 2015

Lilies

"The light multiplied, flew out in all directions.
Like a perfume whose vial had been laid aside
And lost in the bottled-up illusion of the past
Suddenly it seemed to atomize and fill the air...
It filled my thoughts, nothing exempt...
But lilies everywhere...
Lilies of forgiveness, fragrant, endless...
Forgiving me for years of labor,
Mentally and physically attempting to fashion myself
Who was already created...trying to become
When I already Am!"

Excerpt from *An Ordinary Angel Pays a Call...*
by Barbara Arrington
17 September 07

Chapter 1: Prologue

Who Am I, and How Did I Get Here?

God said to Moses, "I AM WHO I AM." He said further, "Thus you shall say to the Israelites, 'I AM has sent me to you.'" Ex 3:14

I AM here because God has sent me
to be who I AM.

It's the first day of the rest of your life, and you just emerged from slumber into that not-quite-awake state with a startling sensation of wonder. Everything feels just slightly different – familiar but different somehow. You go through your normal morning routine with continued wonder, noticing textures and sensations as you do what you do. Scents, sounds, conversations, flavors seem more interesting and exotic as you engage with your world. Activities proceed, and you forget about the newness sensation till finally, as you unwind at the end of the day, you remember the odd sensations of the morning. You ponder the feelings of newness that permeated your morning routine, as though you were living your life with someone else's mind. That's when the big question erupts into your awareness: "Who am I, and how did I get here?"

We know our statistics: name, date of birth, social security number, sex, height, weight, hair color, eye color, marital status, profession, employer, home address, phone numbers, religion, ethnicity, etc. We know ourselves by our roles and relationships. We know

1

ourselves by our causes and commitments. We occupy very specific spaces in our known worlds, and we have an array of ideas about the reality we inhabit. We've spent a lifetime building an external world of connections and experiences, sorted and categorized in memory for future reference. We've amassed a repertoire of emotional reminiscences, some pleasant, others not so much, and a dossier of attitudes towards the world and its events and participants. We live in a self-constructed cocoon of perceptions and interpretations, and we continue to build, strengthen, furnish and ornament our cocoons as we attract and interact with known and unknown elements through observations and direct experiences.

We have questions about our lives and experiences, and we are curious about things we have or haven't seen or experienced yet. Some of us are especially curious about things that can't be investigated directly. Throughout history people have told stories, and discussed and argued, about where we came from, how we got to where we are and where we'll go when we aren't here anymore. Every culture has a lexicon of legends, myths, stories, traditions and mysteries surrounding its origins and perpetuation, its triumphs and tragedies, and the ways humankind can influence the course of human events. Studying the traditions of world cultures reveals myriad dimensions of Origins and Originators, as well as implications that we may all be referring to the same Source for all Creation.

Who hasn't pondered the questions, "Who am I, and how did I get here?"

Source

God is the name many use to describe the ultimate creative power known to humankind. Others use words like Higher Power, Divine Mind, Christ, Buddha, Allah, Jehovah or Yahweh to name the creator of the universe. Some religious traditions see God as transcendent – beyond human awareness or knowing, unnamable and indescribable. Others view God as immanent, active in human affairs and perceptibly present. Regardless of the view we embrace, the tricky part is that defining the energy, consciousness, entity or being that created us requires us to think thoughts that are bigger than our brains. It's like asking a 3-year-old to explain his daddy's job. Daddy may be a senior designer for the next generation of graphics software, but "he makes computer stuff" may be the 3-year-old version. Attempting to define the energy that created us immediately limits and structures the Infinite because defining something makes it finite. Our Creator is infinite and not definable and at the same time is a personal presence.

Because our minds, our physical brains and the chemical/electrical processes that operate them, and our language, made up of nouns and verbs that represent things we know and have experienced, are finite (growing but still finite), we cannot know all of our Source. We can know <u>about</u> it but cannot comprehend its entirety because our conscious minds are contained within it.

But what if we approach conceptualizing our Source, or God, from the inside out? What if we look inside ourselves for evidence of our own primal origin? We all had parents, went to school and perhaps had some religious experiences growing up. Some lucky things happened to us, some unlucky things; our self-assessment may have vacillated from year to year as things went well or not so well. We may have felt the presence of God intensely from time to time or never at all. We may have felt that the Creator had dropped us off here on Earth the day we were born, and we were on our own from there on out. The idea of being a child of God may have been woven into our consciousness, or perhaps we had a sense of God as an ever-present but invisible Parent.

So here's where you need to take a deep breath and just try on the following idea:

Are you alive?
Are you breathing?
Are you conscious?
Do you love someone or something?
Then you are God.

Oh, dear. What a shock. Sorry.
Well, let's back up a bit. The intelligence in you that is reading these words is Divine Intelligence, the same Intelligence that creates the world and everything we experience daily. The warm feeling in your chest when you think of someone special is love, the same Divine Love that harmonizes and smoothes out the bumps and bruises of the world. The sensation of being alive as you breathe in and out is life, the same Divine Life that enlivens every living organism on our planet. The fact that you are alive, you are breathing, you are conscious and you love is proof of your oneness with God. Better still, those conditions are evidence that **God is alive as you**. God is Life. God is Love. God is Consciousness, Intelligence, Creativity, Joy, Peace – every good thing we can imagine. God is Imagination!

God is all, everything – and God is all that is. God is so big and so much that God is neither good nor evil. God just Is.

Remember Moses and the burning bush? "I Am who I Am," said the Voice from the bush that burned but was not consumed by the fire.

Now we have to modify all this by understanding that our "I Ams" have been living in bodies for a while and have been soaking up a lot of external evidence from the outer world the whole time. We probably have a lot of information and ideas that are not quite pristine in their pure divinity. We may even have some religious dogma or attitudes that might be at odds with the total infinite Universal Intelligence that is available to us.

No problem – God can handle all of that. God, remember, created the whole scenario. God started the whole experience for us – not in the traditional seven days of creation, but in the consciousness of one's Being, at the moment that one's consciousness claimed its individual identity. That probably happened sometime before each of us emerged from our mothers' wombs, though we may not remember it. What an ego experience – to think that a mind created by God, inhabiting a body created by God, could actually see itself as separate from God!

Here and Now

"I see you have come up to here." That's a greeting from the tradition of the Hopi tribe, Native Americans who lived atop the mesas in what is now northern Arizona. A visitor would have climbed a steep rocky path to arrive in the village, so acknowledging that arrival was a polite way to begin the conversation. In their spiritual tradition, though, it carried a deeper implication of growth and progress through time and life experience. Have you come up to here? Where is the "here" you've come up to?

5

Near the Hopi reservation in Arizona is the Grand Canyon. When viewed from the rim, the Colorado River is a thin line of silver snaking through the red rock depths of the Canyon. But after hiking down the 7-mile trail to the canyon floor, one can see the river is a wide, swift stream of very cold water. Here and now, from the bank, one can step into the river – but the next time one steps in at the same spot, it's a different river because the water and the moment have flowed on downstream and into the past.

Rafting the Grand Canyon provides another perspective on here and now. One is borne downstream aboard a large rubber raft, passing between steep rock walls or alongside sand banks. Eras of geologic history are visible as the colors of the rock walls become darker. "Here" travels with us on the raft as we pass through the changing scenery of the river's course.

Regardless of whether you're standing on the bank as the river flows past, or you're riding on the raft past the walls of the canyon, here and now is your exact location. No matter where you live or work, no matter what events have transpired thus far or are impending, at this moment you are still here, now. You bear within you the immutable truth of your being, you are who you are, and you are practicing your highest and best expression of your Self in all situations.

Your spiritual standing at this particular point in time is probably different from an earlier status. Not that one is greater or less than another – it's just where you are now. If you're reading this book, you're most likely a spiritual seeker who already has many experiences and realizations under your belt or your hat or up your sleeve, as the case may be.

Many believe that your soul/spirit is eternal and has been around for eons and lifetimes. They believe you've brought into this life experience a memory cache of instincts and attitudes that shape your preferences and modes of expression beneath your conscious awareness. Others believe that this physical existence, beginning with the moment you emerged from your mother's womb and ending with your last exhalation, is all there is. They might say you're dealing with the accumulation of information and experience that you've acquired directly since you've been in this body. Either way, "here and now" is who you are at this moment, which is not exactly the same as who you were 10 minutes ago, nor is it the same as who you will be 10 minutes from now. Knowing oneself intimately is an ongoing project that requires scrupulous honesty and meticulous observation.

Meditation is a great tool in this undertaking because it gives you some perspective on the mind you're using to observe yourself. If you are an experienced meditator, you understand the power of stepping away from the everyday phases of mind – the problem-solving, the critical thinking, the competing, the list-making – and allowing deep inner silence to "reboot" your conscious mind. If you haven't yet experienced the deep inner silence of meditation, you may have experienced a similar sense of renewal after deep immersion in nature, music, art or anything else that takes your mind out of its usual surroundings and thought patterns.

That deep inner silence is where we come into awareness of our spiritual source, the constant touchstone in our spiritual quest. Many of the ideas and impressions we live with, the content of our conscious minds, have been filtered through someone else's consciousness. We've picked up impressions from listening, reading and observing our outer surroundings. These concepts and ideas may work for some parts of our lives but probably won't work for all. Even the ideas you're reading at this moment have come from the author's consciousness, which means they need to be vetted by your highest understanding of truth or ultimate reality. This is your divine right and responsibility because as you live in your world with your understanding of who you are and how you got here, your thoughts, words and actions arise from your highest understanding of ultimate reality.

One's experience of the world is custom-built, constructed according to the habitual expectations and explanations we hold. So "here and now" is fluid, your highest understanding of Truth is growing, and you have a deepening sense of "Who Am I?" and "How Did I Get Here?" The importance of knowing how you got here is mostly so that you can continue to refine your navigation, your habitual expectations and explanations, toward where you want to be.

Wearing the Skin Suit

As a spiritual being having a human experience, you've been wearing a skin suit all your life. A skin suit is actually a kind of costume worn by dancers — like a full-body leotard. But for the purposes of this work, your "skin suit" is your personality/physical body. It's the vehicle that carries your mind/soul/spirit through the day-to-day experiences of living, the outfit or maybe the armor you wear in the world. It emerged from your mother's womb at your birth (wearing what is sometimes referred to as your "birthday suit") and has grown with you through your lifetime. It has suffered some slings and arrows — skinned knees, stubbed toes, the flu, chicken pox, insults or teasing — and has interacted with your environment to the best of its ability (sunburn, calluses, allergies, avoidance or coping mechanisms). It may show the effects of experience, but it has adapted, healed and recovered brilliantly throughout your occupancy.

As a result of having carried your mind/soul/spirit through the adventures of your life up to now, your skin suit may have developed some preferences and aversions. It prefers to be safe, warm and comfortable and is probably averse to anything that appears to threaten that safe, warm comfort. One large category of threat is "Change from Outside," meaning changes that are somebody else's idea. Even when the change is your idea, your skin suit may try to talk you out of it ("yes, I know we need to lose five pounds, but that cupcake is so tiny and looks so delicious, it won't make that big a difference, and we can start over again tomorrow . . .").

Another is "Change from Within," which is the result of realizing a new level of knowing. One begins to live from that new awareness, which may be met with resistance or rebellion from the skin suit or the habits of body or mind. Once again, meditation to the rescue! During meditation, your skin suit gets to relax. Your mind/soul/spirit gets to "unzip the skin suit" and reconnect with its Creator, the Source of Being. The skin suit gets a rest – literally. Your heart rate slows, respiration deepens and regulates, brain waves smooth out . . . a spa experience all around. Your skin suit awakens refreshed and attuned to the Truth of your Being, restored and ready to continue the adventure.

In the theaters of ancient Greece and Rome, actors wore enormous masks with exaggerated features so that even the audience members in the back row could identify their characters' faces. Those masks were called *persona*, and the word came to mean the character played by the actor. In more recent times, *persona* has come to mean a social role, and the personality refers to the complex of characteristics that distinguishes an individual. When we talk about a person's personality, we usually are describing the way that person "shows up" in everyday life as they interact with others and respond to situations. But somehow we sense that there's more to that person, that human being, than the personality we encounter. We occasionally catch a glimpse of a deeper energy coming through as compassion, wisdom, insight or creativity. Something deeply authentic emerges through the surface personality, and we feel we have gotten to know that person a bit better.

There is only one supreme creative power in the Universe. Every living being is a manifestation or expression of that power. That power is infinitely creative, expressing itself in every thought, word or action. When we are born into the world, we don't separate from the universal source or power. We just change the connection or format of the communication or expression. Our conscious awareness is the sensor that connects us to the outer world and to the universal source.

Self

Self is such a small word – only four letters – yet the volumes of commentary on the concept of "self" date back millennia. In many spiritual traditions, the self is considered the mechanism whereby the individual believes that it is separate from God. In some traditions the self is ego; in others, it's the soul or the identity. Simply put, your self is who you are.

It appears that the sense of self as an entity or autonomous being survives severe amnesia and that the sense of self is retained throughout the changes of an individual's life circumstances.

Victims of severe brain trauma still have a sense of being themselves, even though they may have no idea who they are. Individuals who undergo extensive surgery – cosmetic, restorative, organ replacement – are still themselves, with upgraded bodies. People who reinvent themselves after career changes, relocations, divorces or other major events still have a distinct sense of themselves. In fact, they may feel more like themselves than they did before the change!

Consider yourself. What is your identity? Not your name, rank and serial number but your main identity. Who are you? We looked at this at the beginning of this chapter – what did you decide?

When we look in the mirror, it's always the same eyes that look back at us. They're the same eyes that looked back at us when we were young, working out our budding adult identities. No matter how many years we've gazed at those eyes, no matter the changes in the face or hair, the eternal self behind the eyes is still the same.

Science tells us that who we are is the result of two factors: genetics and the environment. Nature and Nurture. Hardware and Software. The physical body is built according to the blueprints encoded in the DNA. The mind is built by the interaction of the physical organism with the environment – literally. Neurological structures in infants are modified by the sensory input generated by the child's actions and experiences in the physical world. The neural pathways that support language or motor skills are built by the experience of the sounds of the child's environment being perceived by the auditory mechanism or by the sensations of moving. The child's cognitive and emotional development is a result of experience in the world, interacting, experimenting and observing the world in which she lives.

The "hardware," the physical body and brain, is built largely by biological functions. The "software," the attitudes and ideas, is created and programmed by the individual's interaction with the environment. The self is the whole which is greater than the sum of its parts – the spirit/soul/body of the human being.

The minute we ask ourselves, "Who am I?" we are attempting to define the self, the infinite being that inhabits our skin suit. As we saw earlier, we can list our descriptors and our roles, the facts and figures of our lives and experiences – but that still begs the question. The point of asking the question is actually to expand the answer, which expands our sense of self, which expands the capacity for actualizing more of the unlimited potential that is ours because we are alive and conscious.

Let's use the earth as a metaphor. We live on the surface of the earth's crust, and we know that the earth's core is composed of heavy metals at incredibly high pressure and temperatures. At its center, the core is a solid mass of a nickel-iron alloy suspended in a liquid layer of molten iron and nickel. Surrounding the core is the mantle, a thick, dense body of magma or semi-molten rock. Magma moves beneath the earth's crust, beneath our feet, and occasionally shifts a section of the crust or surges through an opening in the crust to form new earth. As the magma emerges as lava, it is shaped by the cooler rocks, water and air of the earth's crust and atmosphere. The sinuous emergence of the lava from beneath the earth's crust and the dramatic encounter of the lava with the waters of the Pacific Ocean are sometimes spectacularly visible at the edge of the Kilauea eruption site on the island of Hawaii. New earth emerges continually from magma vents on land and deep beneath the sea. Those heavy metals from the core have emerged, pressed out through the mantle and the crust into view, forming new land.

At the core (from the Anglo-French word for heart) of every human is pure spirit – God – which emerges into expression through words and deeds. As we grow from infancy into adulthood, we develop ways of interacting with our environment and the people in it. We try out ways of communicating and responding, discarding unsuccessful behaviors and refining those that get more satisfactory results. The remaining assortment of preferences, behaviors, ideas and abilities becomes our personalities, or our "skin suits." Because our personalities are the result of interactions among many variables in our genetic makeup as well as in our experience, each is unique and unpredictable. Our choices of action and expression are continuous, moment to moment.

As with a holographic image, all of God's essence is available in individual expression. A fragment of a hologram still produces the whole image. God within every living being, invisible, intangible and immeasurable, is the unconscious, indefinable source of consciousness. It is the irrepressible energy that springs forth as spontaneity and creativity, that reaches out to others as compassion and generosity and that knows itself as wisdom and love. Just as magma emerging from the earth's mantle is shaped by its contact with the earth's crust and atmosphere, the crust and atmosphere are shaped by the emergence of the magma. The expression of spirit is shaped by the mind and body of the individual, and the mind and body are shaped by the expression of spirit.

The self is the expression of God through our thoughts, words and deeds. God, the infinite creative intelligence, emerges through us as our interactions and creations, our work, play and relationships.

13

The impulses that prompt us and the behaviors through which we act on those impulses are the expression of God through us. Each thought, word or deed is a building block of our persona or personality, shaped by the mind and body that express it.

As we continue our quest for Truth, our awareness of self as an expression of the divine deepens, and we more fully express the purity of the Spirit that is our original Source.

All life proceeds from one universal source. The one source is not here and now, in a specific location or at a certain time. It is everywhere, omnipresent and eternal. That source is the true identity of all creation and the common denominator of all humankind. As we grow in our individual expression of the energy of the divine, we purify or sanctify that identity we know as our self. As we expand our expression of spirit, more light and energy become available to be shared among our fellow beings. Imagine yourself as a beacon of light, love, inspiration and hope to all the rest of us!

Who are you, and how did you get here?

I am "I AM" individualized, and
"I AM" has sent me to the world.

Chapter 2

God is Life,
the Animating Essence

In the beginning was the Word, and the Word was with God, and the Word was God. He was in the beginning with God. All things came into being through him, and without him not one thing came into being. What has come into being in him was life, and the life was the light of all people. The light shines in the darkness, and the darkness did not overcome it. John 1:1-5

I am alive and alight as
the individualized Word of God.

The Gospel writers had to work very hard to express in words their new understanding of Spirit, God, the Christ and all the subtle shifts that took place as a result of Jesus's work. The Word is the active power of God, the function of God that <u>said</u>, "Let there be . . ." Other functions of God might be Source (energy or substance) or Universal Mind (wisdom, understanding, creativity), but for now let's just think about God as the Word. The Word, the Active Power of God, created the world, the heavens and the earth, the seas and the dry land, and LIFE. Being alive is what lights all people – the light of Spirit, shining in the darkness and overcoming the darkness.

There's a mysterious quality that science hasn't been able to analyze or identify yet. It's the *something* that animates every living cell on the planet. Some cells are no longer living – that whatever-it-is has "left the building." The physical material of the cell is still there, but when that animating essence departed, the viability of the cell ceased and decay began. Decay isn't bad – it's a law of nature. It's a change in function as part of a natural cycle. Once an organism is no longer alive, its physical materials are reused, repurposed or recycled for the benefit of other living organisms.

So what is that animating essence that sparks the growth and activity of all living organisms? Biologists haven't exactly pinpointed it yet. They don't think it's chemical or electrical, though it certainly affects both chemical and electrical activity. I'm not sure what the technical term would be; some might call it *prana* or *chi* or *mana* or life-energy. But what if it was actually the life force of the Universe, known as God for short?

God Who?

Who or what is this God that everybody talks about? Is God the scary guy in the sky with the beard who knows everything and is the master player of "Gotcha!"? Is God the last resort in times of extreme urgency – "when all else fails, pray!"? Is God the sugar daddy to be wheedled and petitioned for the current heart's desire – "please, God, I'll never ask for anything else!"?

No matter what you think God is, God is more. Because God is infinite, beyond description and quantification, some describe God as Energy. We use energy, we harvest it, and we understand some applications of it.

Energy. Intangible, invisible, infinitely potent and beyond human understanding. Humans have used art and literature throughout human history to portray God in language or imagery, but God is more directly known through experiences or phenomena.

"Miracles," maybe, or unexplainable events are sometimes considered "acts of God" – but nobody really knows how those acts are executed.

So let's turn our telescopes around, using the lenses as microscopes to look at the observable evidence of that invisible, intangible power in our physical world. A tiny seed responds to moisture and warmth by swelling, splitting its husk, extending a tiny fiber out into the environment, drawing in sustenance, swelling some more, opening another crack in the husk, extending a tendril in the opposite direction, drawing in more sustenance, expanding into more fiber and tendrils until it is a mature carrot or oak tree or corn stalk. We're learning more about DNA and genetic encoding, so there's not as much mystery there as before. Not all seeds are "viable"; some don't sprout regardless of the external conditions. So what was the "pilot light" that made that seed viable, made it come to life when planted in the right soil conditions? What's the difference between "alive" and "dead"? God.

Life is defined in the Merriam-Webster Dictionary as "an organismic state characterized by capacity for metabolism, growth, reaction to stimuli, and reproduction." Death is defined as "the absence of life." Simply stated, "alive" means growing, and "dead" means decaying. God is present and active in everything, dead or alive; the difference is simply that live things grow into more of themselves and dead things get repurposed.

God is growth, life and energy. God is the Life in our bodies, the energy that lights each cell and prompts each impulse of our bodies and minds. Basic biology: alive and growing or dead and decaying. We're all part of the Divine economy, feeding and being fed,

17

inhaling and exhaling, expanding and contracting, consuming and contributing.

Animation and Decay

Animation: from the Latin *anima* or soul. That which quickens or brings to life. Alive things are animated, dead ones are not. They have no soul.
If a person dies, his *anima* has departed. The body is no longer animated. The physical organism is no longer being sustained by the life force and thus begins to break down, disintegrate or decay. Depression might be considered a suppression of the *anima*, resulting in diminished life force and thereby initiating disease of the physical organism in tandem with the disease of the mind.

Decay is a process, nature's way of recycling – we already covered that. Destruction is an important part of growth. The Hindu deity Shiva is the God of Destruction, and he is not a bad guy. He cleans things out to make room for new. We have to let go of things that are not for our highest and best. Remember those old favorite running shoes, and how sore your knees got from running on those worn-out soles? A new pair of running shoes makes a huge difference – especially after they're slightly broken in. Closets, kitchens, drawers, garages and basements need to be cleaned out from time to time, and the spaces feel so much lighter and more energetic when it's done. Sustaining things and maintaining them require a lot of energy that might be better spent in creating or enhancing. Of course, creating and enhancing the same things over and over can turn into sustaining and maintaining, at which point we can decide to release and replace – or not.

Composting is my favorite example of the constructive power of decay. Just think of the creative power in your banana peels and coffee grounds! All those organic materials are releasing their nutrients to be transformed into rich, fertile soil, which then works with the minerals in the earth to nurture beautiful, wholesome food, fragrant flowers and zesty herbs. They grow from those powerful little seeds that we appreciated earlier. They're filled with life, the animating essence, another name for God, the "pilot light" mentioned earlier that makes the seed viable.

Not only are human beings alive, but we have consciousness. Consciousness is defined as "the state of being [which is] characterized by sensation, emotion, volition, and thought." The activity of spirit goes beyond consciousness and physical activity. Spiritual animation (almost a redundancy) is the result of God-mind flowing into and through consciousness, usually in prayer, meditation, contemplation, selfless service or other spiritually oriented activity.

Change and Divine Order

Among the lifestyles in humankind, some of us value permanence in the form of houses, roads and cities. Others of us prefer to migrate with the seasons, following nature to homes of natural protection, supply and comfort. Nature is in constant change, with seasons of growth, discarding and resurrection. The physical structures created by man are acted upon by nature, resulting in changes requiring maintenance, which then change the way nature acts upon the structures, and on it goes.

Life and change are inseparable. Change surrounds life, framing it and forming it. Change is constant. Being animated results in change, either growth or decay. Diminished animation leads to diminished growth and ultimately to decay.

Change embraces repetition but has no respect for duplication. Repetition produces change in the repeater as well as in the repeated. Change continues when animation has ceased. Resisting change requires great energy and is ultimately futile. Embracing and dancing with change transforms energy and creates powerful opportunities for growth and progress. It affirms animation, creating powerful opportunities for growth and progress.

Change can rarely be controlled. It can sometimes be managed, negotiated or mitigated, but the universe is too complex to allow isolation of change from all factors. Aside from a strictly controlled scientific laboratory, there's always room for a surprise or an unexpected twist. That's why no one can ever know what's going to happen next. Then guided by our spiritual intuition, we imagine, create and innovate to successfully navigate the changes presented by circumstances and choice.

Divine order is the process by which, and the reassurance that, all things work together for good. Divine order is the organizing activity of Spirit that works with the perceptive, creative individual mind to manifest the highest and best for all concerned. Divine order is a multitude of tiny actions, doing just the next right thing. Consciousness sets divine order in motion when we access our intuition by turning away from appearances toward our inner knowing. The reason divine order works is that God is omnipotent. When we look back on a surprisingly positive outcome to what had appeared to be certain disaster, divine order is the amazing, invisible complex of intelligent energy that pulled it all together. Cooperating with and participating in divine order requires faith and perseverance, nurtured by regular times in deep silence to reestablish conscious connection with God.

The breath is the source and entrance to the creative Mind. As we consciously breathe, we return to awareness of our connection with our Creator, and we remember how to dance with change. As we dance with change, we create the effects and results of change in our lives, and Divine Order is re-established. To breathe and dance with change is to be fully alive, fully one with God and fully at peace.

Forgiveness: Getting Back on Track

Forgiveness is how we reunite with God in all Creation. Forgiveness is meaningless unless we have judged. God does not judge because God is all. We judge and condemn, so we need to forgive ourselves and others in order to return to wholeness/holiness. Forgiveness has nothing to do with others. It is done for the benefit of one's inner Self, to release it from the constricting energy of having judged and to reconnect with the Creator in all creation.

The Universe is plastic and malleable. Our "judgment" names and shapes our experience and our path. When we choose to name all things good, to dance with changes and grow through them to make the most of our flow of divinity, our capacity for divine energy is increased, and we are more aligned with our creative power.

The life force surges through us non-stop, 24/7/365. When we're "in the flow," we feel the power and clarity of our aliveness as we do what we do with assurance and exhilaration. Even when we take a break and relax a bit – a book, a nap, a game of tennis – the life force surges through us as renewal, re-creation. The only thing that

21

derails the life force is judgmental criticism or calling something bad.

Our awareness of our responsibility for our actions is good. Think about it. God, the life force, the universal creator and sustainer of all that is, looked at God's creation at the end of each day and called it good. Who are we to look at anything and call it not good? Who are we to criticize and judge ourselves and others?

We can't be mindless, indiscriminate rubber-stamp okayers of all we see – but our judgment will be much more meaningful and constructive if we start with finding the good in that which we feel moved to criticize. A gardener affirms the beauty and life in the shrub before pruning away the excess growth; a sculptor envisions the form and balance of the statue before chiseling away the excess stone.

Anne Davies, an educational coach in British Columbia, once shared a process for authentically critiquing students' work. She had successfully incorporated peer reviews in her classroom by asking students to comment on classmates' work, using a formula for their remarks. The formula was "Two Compliments and a Wish." Each reviewer was to find two elements of the work to compliment – specific, meaningful compliments such as "your detailed illustration of the thoracic cavity clarified your explanation of the function of the lungs and diaphragm," or "your sensitive articulation made the lyrics of your song more powerful and clear." Then the reviewer was to suggest one improvement to the work: "I wish you would say more about how levers and fulcrums made construction of the Egyptian pyramids possible." Somehow, hearing two things that were successful made the presenters more receptive to hearing criticism. It made them feel that their work was valued and was worthy of further effort.

What does this have to do with forgiveness? Well, suppose that you find yourself marching along through a normal day of effective activity, being your glorious self in your divinely ordered world, divine life surging through your every thought, word and action. Suddenly, your creative, purposeful flow of activity is interrupted by an event that seems counterproductive. Perhaps a traffic jam, a copier jam, a misunderstanding with a co-worker or a tardy appointment disturbs the calm peace of your soul. You feel the wind dropping out of your sails, your energy sags, and the onslaught of negative emotions begins.

Complaints surface in droves. Blame arrives, demanding to be laid at someone's door – maybe your own, maybe that of a specific individual, maybe over a whole organization. This downward spiral of life energy is like that of an aircraft having suddenly lost all engine power – a nosedive out of the altitude of creative activity. How to stop it and pull up? Forgiveness!

Forgiveness has nothing to do with anyone else. You don't have to go make up with the copier or apologize to the person who was the target of your meltdown in traffic. You need to forgive – give yourself a break, give the offending party a break – by somehow sucking up your inner fortitude and coming up with a compliment or two for your universe and your situation. Hit the "pause" button, and freeze the action on your mental screen.

The Institute of HeartMath teaches the techniques of "Freeze Frame" and "Heart Lock-In," and this is the time to apply them. "Freeze Frame" is exactly that – the "pause" button on your mental video player. Stop the action, stop thinking about it, just hold everything. Then change your focus by doing a "Heart Lock-In": direct your attention inward to pure unconditional love – your dog's enthusiastic greeting, your baby's sweet snuggling, your garden's fragrant flowers – anything that makes you smile and remember who you really are. Hold your attention in the "Heart Lock-In" until its warmth, love and joy have washed away the tension and stress of whatever set you off.

Take a deep breath and let it out, give yourself one last dose of unconditional sweetness, and then mentally offer a sip of that sweetness to the person you came so near to judging. Whew – that was close! You almost shot yourself in the foot by judging, but you recovered beautifully.

Now that you're safely back in your loving, centered, purified, original self, try beholding that other person as a child struggling with a load too heavy. Could you respectfully offer assistance? Would some quiet space to recover be a gift of love to the other? You are whole, well, creative and resilient, and nothing can disturb the calm peace of your soul. The life force is flowing freely within you, and you are once again in harmony with yourself and all of creation. You have demonstrated that forgiveness is giving life energy instead of withdrawing it. Even when one has been devastated by what appears to be the senseless destruction of something precious, forgiveness restores the beauty of the memory and the inner experience of that preciousness.

Infants who are deprived of snuggling fail to thrive. Situations deprived of life energy fail to resolve. Injuries deprived of life energy fail to heal. To forgive is to recharge, consciously and deliberately, the life energy in yourself with regard to any given experience, relationship, situation or event. Forgiveness opens your personal valve for an infusion of Divine life throughout the system – whether it be physical, emotional or relational. It is intensely personal and completely internal, taking place in the privacy of your mind and heart. Forgiveness is the instant repair kit for punctures of the soul, sealing the energy leak from within and re-inflating your being to its normal buoyant state.

Genesis doesn't give us details of the obstacles God may have encountered in the process of creating the earth and its inhabitants, but what if there were issues along the way? No biggie – God is omnipotent, you say. God can just say "Let there be . . .," and there it would be. The life force, the divine energy, would continue to flow through the creative process. As children of God, we can do the same thing. Forgiveness is that special application of life force used for cleansing and restoring damaged circumstances to full-speed-ahead creativity and joy.

As we saw earlier, forgiveness is important in promoting full flow of the life force in and through ourselves and our lives. Unforgiveness – holding a grudge – siphons off a portion of our life force. Add unforgiveness to physical damage – illness or an injury – and the flow of life force can really get reduced. At some point the organism may not be able to sustain life anymore and just shut down. At that point the life force is gone, and decay can set in, clearing away the usable bits and repurposing others. It's an extreme example, but if you had to choose to either forgive or decay, how long would you have to think about it?

God's Life is limitless and fully available all the time. God created you and me and all the rest of us; we share the same life force and the same spiritual light. Keep breathing, keep forgiving, and keep shining because your light overcomes the darkness every moment of every day!

**With each breath I forgive, and
my light shines ever brighter
as it overcomes the darkness.**

Chapter 3
God is Love,
the Attracting Energy

Jesus answered, "The first is, 'Hear, O Israel: The Lord our God, the Lord is one; you shall love the Lord your God with all your heart, and with all your soul, and with all your mind, and with all your strength.' The second is this, 'You shall love your neighbor as yourself.' There is no other commandment greater than these." Mark 12: 29

I enfold my neighbor and myself in my wholehearted love as God-beings.

Think about the deepest, most powerful experience of love you've ever known. Go back through the history of your days and months, through the eras of your life. It might have been love shared with a pet, a parent, a child, a friend, a community. You may have been giving love to another or receiving love from another. You've probably had numerous experiences of love throughout your life, under different circumstances and in various relationships.

Life seems somewhat more quantifiable than love. There's been some scientific exploration around the nature and functioning of the essence we know as life. Life can be measured as chemical or electrical activity. Love, however, has inspired significantly more art, music and poetry, probably because we have to describe it since we don't really know how to measure it.

We know that life can leave a physical being. When it does, we call its departure or absence death. But can love vacate us? There have certainly been times when we have experienced the loss of love from a particular person or relationship. The quality and effect of love can change – can deepen or lessen. We can experience loneliness – is that the absence of love? But even in loneliness, when we feel unloved, we can still feel love for another – perhaps a distant or inaccessible other, but still a beloved other. That's because love is perceived and experienced through one's consciousness, perhaps prompted by a memory, but not dependent on the physical presence of the beloved.

The absolute truth is that God is omnipresent and God is love; therefore, there can never be an absence of love. We may not be able to feel it or perceive it, but it is there as the cohesive energy that draws us onward and forward, toward our next connection and opportunity.

Love, Hate and Fear

God is love. I am a child of God; therefore, I am love as well. Fear and hatred have nothing to do with me because I live, move and have my being immersed in and permeated by Divine Love. Love is my nature, and gratitude is my gift.

Hatred is such an unpleasant word. The emotion is intensely negative, destructive and threatening, yet the activity of hating is as much a commitment as loving. How can this be, that hating binds as firmly as loving? Because of the intense energy expended in the process of hating. It takes a lot of energy to be relentlessly antagonistic, no matter how cherished the antagonism. Acting on hatred fuels the flames of pain, anger and unforgiveness.

Retribution triggers revenge, and the destructive cycle can spiral into total annihilation. The battle may go dormant temporarily, but the energy remains, and the anger can erupt anew – unless the energy is shifted and transformed, restored by the intention of Consciousness to Divine purity. Forgiveness is the tool which, grounded in Divine Love for self and other, performs this transformation.

Some might say that hate is the opposite of love. Others might observe the intense involvement of either hate or love and say that they are two sides of the same coin, while apathy, the absence of emotion, is the opposite of either love or hate. *A Course in Miracles*, published by the Foundation for Inner Peace, teaches that the opposite of love is fear. A brilliant scholar, Dr. Jerry Jampolsky, tells us that "love is letting go of fear."

Love is the ultimate strength, the infinite power that stands in the face of all fear and is triumphant. While hatred is an engagement of negative emotion, fear is a defense against perceived hostility. To engage with something is to acknowledge it, to interact with it, to come to terms with it. To defend against something is to avoid it, to deflect its influence, to disengage from it. We established early on that God is love; therefore, while hatred is a destructive application of energy, fear is an avoidance of energy perceived as destructive. Hatred is a perversion of, and fear is a denial of, one's own Divine power.

The idea of hatred being a perversion of Divine power may be antithetical to some. We work diligently to release and heal negative thoughts. Divine power cannot be perverted – it is absolute and immutable. But because we have free will and are created in the image and likeness of God, we are capable of applying Divine power with destructive intentions. That's where the idea of sin comes from – making a mistake. An accidental, unintentional mistake seems less menacing than a deliberate, malicious misdeed, but the bottom line is that they are both mistakes. They are actions that generate kindred reactions because of the spin our intentions put on the energy.

Can love and fear be experienced simultaneously? They can certainly intensify one another, as in the case of a terrified mother protecting her endangered child. But can we love and fear the same thing at the same time? The two are energetic opposites. We can experience them in rapid succession, which is exhausting and cannot be sustained. They will subside just as a storm passes, played out as conditions evolve.

Love amplifies positive energy, fear blocks it and hate repels it. Even when love points out a need for change or correction, it provides the positive energy to encourage growth through the process of change or correction. When fear points out a need for change, it paralyzes by withholding the energy needed. When hate points out a need for change, it destroys by corrupting the energy needed for the change.

Managing one's attitude is a thought-by-thought endeavor. It doesn't have to be – we can just let the thoughts follow the path of least resistance and make the best of whatever results show up. But if we find that the results are not satisfactory, we have to take responsibility for marshaling those thoughts into channels that bear a closer resemblance to our desired results.

Actions taken in love are adaptable – there are many right ways to be loving and creative. Actions taken in love are productive because the driving force is growth and life. A course of action prompted by love will eventually have the desired effect because love is Divine creative energy. The same course of action prompted by fear will starve the desired effect because fear constricts and withholds creative energy. The same course prompted by hate will have a destructive effect – on the instigator as well as the subject – because hate consumes and perverts creative energy. Whatever action you take, be sure that it springs from pure, unconditional love with no reservations, limits or caveats.

But what to do if you are so unbalanced by the intensity of your emotions that you can't find the love in your mind or heart? Give thanks for something – anything – and allow the flow of love within you to restart.

Grace and Gratitude

Gratitude comes from the Latin *gratia*, meaning "grace." Grace refers to events that seem beyond luck, beyond miraculous, as in "by the grace of God." "Saying grace" means giving thanks, usually before eating a meal. Grace is an unearned blessing; it is love in action – the omnipotent and eternal activity of God's love for creation. A "grace period" means a gift of time – often before a payment is considered delinquent and subject to penalty – from a creditor to a debtor. The payee gives the payer a break by allowing a few extra days to fulfill the obligation.

Grace is the gift. Gratitude is the love it engenders. What does gratitude have to do with love?

Gratitude is love in action. Expressing our gratitude is usually associated with having received something good, something we

31

love or appreciate. To appreciate is to increase in value, to become more precious. Take a moment to feel appreciation or gratitude for something around you.   Notice the feeling of expansion and comfort? You might even notice a slight surge of something that feels like love.

Gratitude is the accelerator that amplifies the vibration of good in our lives. Gratitude magnetizes our good to us, drawing all good things from the "ethers," the unlimited, invisible substance of God, into manifestation in our lives. Love and gratitude are like breathing in and out, receiving and giving blessings. They complement each other, each enhancing the depth and power of the other.

Gratitude is the currency of love. The expression of gratitude is an act of loving. Loving prompts appreciation, being loved prompts thankfulness. There seems to be a cyclical relationship in which love and gratitude swirl around each other, amplifying each other's intensity.   Loving someone, caring for them, enjoying their uniqueness and savoring their companionship result in an experience that can only be expressed as gratitude.

By the grace of God, tradition has it, we are forgiven for our mistakes or sins. Because God's love is infinite and eternal, there is nothing we can do to alter or change God's love for us. Because our divine heritage is free will, we have dominion over our choices, our actions and the consequences thereof.

The grace of God is our assurance that we will never need to be forgiven by God because God doesn't judge. Sometimes we judge and even condemn ourselves, so drawing upon the grace of God is very comforting when we need to forgive ourselves. The grace of God is another name for the unconditional Divine Love that makes the infinite wisdom of our Creator immediately and completely available to us as we grow through experiencing the authentic consequences of our choices and actions.

Healing and Regeneration

Regeneration is the healing power of love. The expression of love and gratitude is often prescribed as part of a healing or wellness regimen. What does love have to do with health?

Cells are alive. The life in the cell is divine life. Just as a petri dish in a laboratory is lined with agar to nourish the cells being cultured, love is the food on which life grows. Science has informed us that within the molecules in the cell, subatomic particles respond to observation in accordance with the intention or expectation of the observer. Directing love to the cells of the body, regularly and over time, can support the proper functioning of the cells, tissues and organs, as well as the thoughts, feelings and actions of the individual.

We know that love and life are closely woven; we know that life is enhanced by love. We are living, breathing proof of the power of love to heal and regenerate our physical bodies. Somehow, a mass of cells attracts a soul – or perhaps a soul prompts the massing of the cells – and before you know it, a child is born. The body is a manifestation of consciousness; physical life is the manifestation of divine love as molecules are arranged in such a way as to kindle animation.

The processes of conception and gestation are well documented. The stages of human growth and development have been mapped out over decades of research and observation, but still we don't really know the mechanics of the soul's relationship with the body. We do know that thousands of cells die every day and are replaced by new ones. We also know that every seven years, we have entirely new cells throughout our physical beings, and we live in our continuously renewed and regenerated bodies with love and gratitude. Our souls are served by our bodies with amazing efficiency and grace, for which we are grateful.

The Institute of HeartMath has conducted carefully controlled scientific research for many years into the effects of caring and compassion on the human immune system. Their studies have measured the levels of an antibody known as secretory IgA, found in saliva and throughout the body. Over decades of study, they have consistently reported findings of significantly improved immune functioning following experiences of caring and compassion. Love is healing – literally. When we love or are loved, our bodies heal.

His Holiness Sri Sri Ravi Shankar, founder of the Art of Living Foundation, travels the world to build peace and "put the smile back on the face of humanity." His followers practice a powerful process of breathing, meditation and compassionate service that is taught worldwide to reduce stress and promote well-being. His gentle, playful and compassionate message is one of love and wisdom, affirming the divine in all.

Love frees and magnifies the life force in the body. Being loved opens the channels of healing energy, allowing each cell to do its work. Loving one's self and appreciating one's "skin suit" establishes a climate of self-care and well-being that supports purposeful, dynamic, effective living through all the days of one's life.

Being in pain can be a fearful experience. We respond to pain in one part of the body by holding tension in other parts. The free flow of energy, just when it's needed for healing, is restricted by tension. Being fearful holds healing at bay, postponing the efficacy of the life force working in the cells. The activity of love is blocked by fear, which restricts the nurturance of divine healing light in the body.

The body is the temple of the soul and deserves devoted, careful tending and nurturing. Carrying the soul and spirit through the adventures we call life can take a toll on the body, resulting in injury or disease. Loving the body, appreciating its strength and beauty, promotes healing and regeneration to offset the stresses and damage of the environment.

Attraction and Oneness

Love is the original power of attraction. Love is seeing, recognizing and honoring the Creator in another. Unconditional love opens the door to communion, offering safety, acceptance and oneness. Love offers a commitment to care for, support and nurture.

Feeling attraction is an invitation to love. Not to possess, but to receive. Not to own, but to care for. Feeling attraction is actually a signal that something is missing – something for which your heart already has a space reserved. The disclaimer in small print on this concept, however, is that one size may not fit all. The object of one's current desire may be a reasonable facsimile, almost but not quite right. We may not be able to imagine the actual object or event yet because we've never experienced anything like it. Naming the desire can limit its fulfillment; the ideal fulfillment comes in the form of the divine equivalent. We don't have to know exactly what's in the package – we trust that it's perfect because it's from our infinitely loving Source. The divine equivalent is that which fits the reserved space so perfectly that it slips comfortably into place, with ease and grace, joy and peace.

Ultimately, attraction begets oneness – if we hold the high watch and keep our hearts stayed on God. Living in conscious oneness with God keeps our hearts open to fuller oneness with another. The energy of longing or desire is the impetus to oneness. Love is the active ingredient that assures the fulfillment of our desires. Knowing that our desires are divine portents of our highest and best blessings, we can enfold them in our purest love and hold them close while we follow their guidance towards manifestation.

Holding anything in love is a powerful exercise in mindfulness and commitment. In relationships disappointment and irritation can lead us to withdraw in order to protect ourselves. We become distracted from seeing the divine that drew us to the Beloved in the first place. Forgiveness and appreciation vibrate at a higher frequency than disappointment or irritation, allowing us to restore the harmony of the relationship and grow into greater love and fulfillment. Holding our desires in love allows us to grow into their fulfillment safely, knowing that the purest form of the desire already lives in our consciousness and cannot be imitated or duplicated by false idols.

When we experience or express gratitude, we are imitating God. When we appreciate something, we are calling it good, just as God did in the creation story. We are behaving in a Godly manner. We are acting from our highest selves, the pure original selves. Gratitude provides the training wheels for our consciousness, supporting our habits of thought as they return to oneness with divine mind. Remembering to be grateful, to give thanks, to appreciate and to honor transforms our attitudes and revolutionizes our experiences in life. Conditioning our consciousness by consistently being thankful will shift our perception ever so slightly with each repetition, refocusing our views of the world one tiny click at a time until we are in awe of the magnificence of Creation all the time.

The secret of all this is that when we couple love with gratitude, we find that our desires have already been fulfilled! Adopting an "attitude of gratitude" in love, with every thought, transforms our desires into blessings.

Love is the glue that holds Creation together. This synergy of love and gratitude, shared between the Creator and the Created, bind us into Oneness and Wholeness. Jesus told us how much God loves us, and how we are to love God. The Gospel writers' messages at the beginning of the chapter are expressed in the language of two thousand years ago. Perhaps in 21st century terms, the message might be understood thus:

My gratitude for God's love for me
assures me of grace.
My love for God and God's Creation is my identity.

Chapter 4
Behold the Lilies

"Behold the lilies of the field, how they grow; they neither toil nor spin, yet I tell you, even Solomon in all his glory was not clothed like one of these." Mt. 6:28-29

I blossom in the assurance of my rightful place
in God's abundant creation.

Are you not worth more than the lilies? That was Jesus's next question in the Sermon on the Mount. His point was that we have much more important work than toiling or spinning or worrying about what we will eat or what we will put on. Our work is to seek the Kingdom of God, which probably looks a lot like the high-end version of the Garden of Eden but is more directly experienced as flourishing in spiritual oneness with our Creator.

Prosperity is the birthright of every living thing. You are a creation of the original creator of the universe, and your sustenance is assured. Your presence in creation is a gift and a blessing for which creation shows its appreciation by surrounding you with abundance in all good things.

You are an integral component in a carefully balanced environment, supporting and being supported by other integral components. As you offer your gifts, you are showered with gifts. The lilies of the field, the violets of the woods, the daisies of the meadows, the geraniums of the window boxes offer their beauty and fragrance to passers-by out of the perfection of their nature. Theirs is to take root, grow, bud, bloom and fade. Yours is to be born, grow, learn, be, love and live out your days in spiritual oneness with your Creator, flourishing as the unique and precious being that you are.

Of course, your physical needs are somewhat more sophisticated and extensive than those of the lilies. A divine order thing, that. Blooming where one is planted is a very good thing for a lily and often so for a person. But sometimes transplanting is required, or dividing or pruning. We love driving along highways strewn with wildflowers, and we admire the colorful beds of annuals at the entrances to apartment complexes. We treasure the natural and cultivated beauties of our botanical gardens and parks. This natural beauty has been helped along by wise and gentle tending.

Your unique and precious Self, the powerful embodiment of the Divine as you, is infinitely capable of attracting all the elements necessary to survive and thrive in this world. Your presence in the world is needed to complete Creation. How could you ever think that the Universe would not support you?

Apparently some of us doubt our indispensability to our world. Some of us think that perhaps it wouldn't matter if we sat this one out. Or perhaps that, really, it wouldn't matter if we slipped through the cracks of society. Some of us might think that we have nothing to offer that is worthy of food, clothing and shelter. We fear that if we relax for a moment, we will be stripped of all our security and protection, abandoned to be blown away by the winter wind.

There is a great need of food, shelter and clothing for a large number of our brothers and sisters around the world today. Many nearer to us here at home are in dire straits and desperately seeking some kind of aid or assistance. Thank goodness for generosity, caring and outreach; thank goodness for the kind hearts of all those who are called to minister and tend to those in need. But just for the sake of conversation, what if those who live in need on the earth, those incredibly brave and generous souls, actually volunteered to do so, to provide an opportunity for others to grow by serving and caring for them?

Extremity has been a challenge among human societies for centuries. Finally, for the first time in the history of humankind, we have the technology and resources to feed all the people on earth. If only we had the willingness!

If ending world hunger or eradicating AIDS or providing fresh drinking water is your calling, you will be supported in making it happen. You will, by following your divine guidance and inner knowing, be led to amazing, miraculous success in fulfilling your destiny by answering your calling. Even more important, you will be fed, clothed and sheltered beyond your expectations by the same universal power that created you and got you this far.

As you walk your path in integrity with your divine guidance, honoring the divine in all you meet, sharing your light in your words and actions, you are blooming where you are planted. You may at some point find yourself being transplanted or pruned or divided, but you will continue blooming with even greater effect as you adapt to your new conditions and flourish, impelled by the power of God in you.

Clothed in Glory

The lilies are clothed more beautifully than Solomon, the wise and wonderful King, in all his glory. Really? And they don't have to toil or spin? Jesus's remarks in the *Sermon on Mount* were intended to encourage His listeners to strive first for the Kingdom of God and not to worry about details like food and clothing because God would feed and clothe them. "Behold how they grow," He says. They're naturally beautiful, naturally wondrous, naturally perfect as lilies, and just by being so, their existence is justified and supported by God as Mother Nature.

Of course, after He had left the earth plane and the disciples were on their own, some of the less enlightened followers decided that meant they could just hang out in Thessalonica and live on the largesse of the wealthier followers of Jesus's teachings. The Apostle Paul had some stern words for them, along with his beautiful words about what love is. We're still trying to figure this out. How do we seek first the Kingdom of God and be assured that all these things like food, drink, clothing and shelter will be added to us as well? Don't we have to have jobs so we can earn a living?

Back to the lilies. Lilies, like all plants, have a very definite place in the plant kingdom. They have jobs to do in the ecosystem. For example, daylilies are really good at holding the soil on a hillside to prevent erosion. Their bulbs are hardy and stubborn, and they cling to that hillside like a network of little sponges, soaking up the water that threatens to wash the whole thing downstream. They stand by through the dry, hot months, bravely waiting for the rains to come again. They bloom exuberantly in their season in a profusion of warm, sunshiny colors, and their graceful leaves soften the

42

landscape while they photosynthesize sunlight and nutrients to make their own food.

So what can you do? Not photosynthesis, certainly, but a lot of other things. As a part of the human ecosystem, you have a job to do. Not your employment, necessarily, but a function to perform. Maybe more than one during the course of your lifetime. It's easy for lilies – they don't really have much choice other than to bloom where they're planted. Humans spend an enormous amount of time, money and energy exploring, seeking, training for and pursuing their life's work. But aren't we supposed to seek first the Kingdom of God? What is the Kingdom of God, and how do you know when you've found it?

The infinite variety in the human race must be a perennial delight for God. God probably gets a big thrill from watching the countless ways we amuse, entertain, irritate and frustrate ourselves and each other with our antics, foibles and eccentricities. We take ourselves and our activities very seriously, and we invest significant amounts of energy in their pursuit. The intense power of our deep engagement in activity – physical, mental, artistic, athletic, curative or whatever – is somewhat akin to the intense power of meditation.

The Hungarian psychologist Mihaly Csikszentmihalyi introduced his concept of "flow" in 1990. He said that people are happiest when they are experiencing "flow," which he explains as a state in which people are so involved in an activity that nothing else seems to matter. In order to experience flow, we need to be working in the "challenge sweet spot" – the degree of difficulty that is just challenging enough to keep us tantalized, engaged and almost but not quite satisfied. Athletes, artists and gardeners experience flow in their chosen activities. People who love what they do are probably also in love with the state of flow, which they achieve by doing whatever they love to do.

What do you love to do? It's very likely that the things you love to do are things you do incredibly well. It's also likely that the few things you don't do so well are things you don't like so much. Wouldn't it be cool if the things you're really good at, the things you love to do, turned out to be exactly what you needed to do to fulfill your life's purpose and experience the Kingdom of God?

Your original core self is multi-talented and extremely adaptable. You have a vast array of possibilities from which to create your personal vision for your life's purpose. There are probably a lot of things you do pretty well, a couple of things you don't do so well, and several things you do incredibly well. Throughout your years, you have been engaged in a wide assortment of activities and endeavors. Your skill set is an amazing collection of know-how and information gained through those activities and endeavors. You may not realize that some of the skills you take for granted are rare and precious and deeply needed by the rest of the world.

Let's take this a step further. What if your particular assortment of talents, abilities, skills and preferences were the result of God being expressed through the body and brain that were hardwired and the mind and heart that were pre-programmed to be you? Wouldn't that be an indication that those talents, abilities, skills and preferences were the raw materials you needed to embody and carry out your life purpose? Wouldn't achieving that exquisite balance of expression and energy be something like experiencing the Kingdom of God?

Take a deep breath, and let it out. It's entirely possible that your life purpose, as a part of your view of the world and how the world works, is about to be re-defined. Of course, being created in the image and likeness of God, you have complete free will in the development and application of these raw materials. Commitment to spirit is your quality control here. It assures the standards of purity that prevent the intrusion of outer influences, and it guarantees the integrity of spirit in your work. Your pure, original self can proceed with its full actualization confidently and serenely with no fear of damage from hurt, disappointment or criticism because God-in-you is greater than anything in the outer world.

Seeking the full actualization of your original self is the same as seeking the Kingdom of God. The full and complete expression of your unique talents, skills, abilities and preferences in fulfilling your life purpose is the greatest gift you can give to humankind, your contribution to the divine order of the universe. So where do you start?

Dreams and Desires

What we see and experience is nothing compared to what we can manifest and create. Your dreams and desires are hints from the Divine that there is yet more in you. That longing in your heart, perhaps even discontent, is the same urge that prompts the chick to peck through the shell of its egg. It's almost as if that desire, longing or discontent is the notice you receive when your order has shipped – the universe is letting you know that you need to expect the arrival of your dream-come-true and head for the post office to pick it up!

This gets a little tricky when we begin to define our desires because we can only interpret them in terms of our prior experience. If we feel a longing or a desire, we feel a need to define or identify that which will satisfy it. But sometimes we name the object of our longing based on what we've already known or experienced. When we place an order from an old catalogue, we may find ourselves disappointed that the item isn't quite what we wanted after all.

Rather being an indication of a need to be filled from the warehouse of past experience, a feeling of longing or desire might be considered a hint or clue. It might actually be a preview of coming attractions with details too fantastic to be understood at present. A desire for change can be the impetus for change in routine or direction, drawing us toward our good along a path we've never traveled.

Maintaining the integrity of a spiritual practice is vitally important to the authenticity of one's dreams and desires because, as we discussed earlier, the impressions of the outer world can result in manufactured dreams and desires as substitutes for the authentic article or experience. But the magnificent thing about your core self is that it can spot an imposter a mile away. Jesus went to the desert on several occasions. He withdrew to a distant, barren place away from his disciples and His thoughts and feelings, to suspend the activity of thinking. In meditation, that vacuum of emptiness, one can be filled with the assurance of one's authenticity and the potent intimacy of one's core self.

Think about a favorite dish that your mom or grandma made. Someone else could make a similar recipe and even serve it in mom's casserole dish, and you'd know. It just isn't quite right. Your original core self is expert at drawing to you exactly what is needed to satisfy that longing in your heart. It supports you and encourages you as you travel the path towards your highest and best. It fans the flame of the dream and keeps it real and alive in your heart. It suggests detours that result in richer experiences and fuller understandings.

Your original core self is the conduit that assures your prosperity through the fulfilling of your dreams and desires. Because your original core self is fully open and receptive to divine instruction and guidance, you are an integral part of the divine order network of universal harmony. We defined divine order earlier as "the organizing activity of Spirit that works with the perceptive, creative individual mind to manifest the highest and best for all concerned." The idea of a network of universal harmony is an embellishment on divine order – imagine a web of energies supporting harmonious growth throughout the universe. You give and receive blessings just as you inhale and exhale. Plants really appreciate your exhalations – they need the carbon dioxide. Your planetmates really appreciate your efforts and results – your creative contributions are exactly what somebody else has been praying for. How cool is that – making your dreams come true answers the prayers of a whole lot of other folks!

Spirit doesn't waste energy. If something is good for you, you are happier and more energized. You have the "juice" to get out there and do what's yours to do. As you fulfill your divine purpose in the world, you nurture the spirit in those who are blessed by the work you've done, the contribution you've made. You "pay it forward," to borrow a term from a beautiful film.

Just imagine the avalanche of good in the world as more individuals start fulfilling their divine purposes, living from the power of Spirit within, blooming where they are planted. They'll be "paying it forward," passing along their passion for life and love as they live their dreams and fulfill their desires, and we'll all be a lot closer to experiencing the Kingdom of God on a daily basis.

A wise man I know observed that when the tide comes in, all the boats are lifted up. When the rain falls, all the flowers get watered. When Spirit is affirmed, all the souls are lifted up. Abundance is universal and infinite. Celebration is contagious. How many times have you joined the wait staff in a restaurant singing "Happy Birthday" to someone you've never met and improvising "dear Hm-mm" because you don't know her name? And didn't you grin at your companions with a bit of glee at having shared the fun?

Dreams and desires are the energy that impels us towards being more of whom we came to be. Let your world celebrate your dreams and desires – let all of us shoot off the fireworks because you are blooming profusely, wherever you are!

Obstacles and Adversities

Let's go back to the idea of transplanting, pruning and dividing. Lilies grow in clumps, sending long spears of leaves up from bulbs under the soil. Healthy lily plants reproduce by making new bulbs in their clumps. Eventually, each clump gets pretty crowded, and there aren't enough nutrients to support all those bulbs, leaves and flowers. So the gentle gardener carefully digs up the clump, tenderly divides it into smaller clumps by loosening the tangle of roots and then replants the new smaller clumps in freshly loosened and amended soil.

48

Other plants may grow so vigorously that they develop straggly branches or so many branches that the roots can't pull in enough nutrients to make healthy leaves or flowers. That's when the gentle gardener brings out the perfectly sharpened pruning shears and very carefully snips off just the right amount of growth in just the right place to encourage healthy new growth.

Sometimes a plant starts out blooming beautifully where it is planted but grows too large for the space. Or perhaps the gentle gardener realizes it will bloom even more beautifully in another spot. The new bed is prepared carefully, with a spacious new planting hole and richly amended soil ready. The plant is lifted from its previous bed, with great care to protect its roots and stem, and then placed tenderly in its new home with the rich soil tucked snugly around its roots. After a few days of careful watering, its leaves perk up, and soon it's blooming more beautifully than ever.

Adversity for a plant sometimes comes in the form of environmental stress – heat, drought, ice, pollution. An overnight freeze leaves our pansies looking pitiful – wilted and soggy – but after a few hours of daylight, they're fresh and cheerful as ever. It's what they do – recover from adversity and keep blooming. The human spirit is every bit as resilient as a pansy; we just have to refrain from talking ourselves out of our own recovery by reliving the drama or holding the grudge.

Obstacles and adversities present opportunities for pruning, dividing and transplanting. Our gentle gardener is, of course, the divine intelligence that guides and inspires us. The process of being pruned, divided or transplanted can be exhausting, painful or frightening. But just as the plant accepts the water, sun and new soil to resume its growth and its blooming, our spirit draws energy and inspiration, strength and courage to continue being and doing that which is ours to be and do. Meditation opens the conduit, allowing energy and inspiration to flow from the Creator to nourish our minds and hearts. Contemplation of that which is good, strong, wise or beautiful refocuses our vision. Selfless service stimulates the growth of deeper, stronger roots of compassion and understanding, and gratitude amplifies the magnetic field drawing greater good to all.

Alignment

Automobiles need to have their wheels aligned from time to time. When the wheels are out of alignment, controlling the direction of travel requires much more effort and energy. When the wheels are aligned correctly, the car goes straight ahead with little steering effort on the part of the driver. How's your inner alignment? What are the standards or values with which you are aligned?

Rotary International serves not only on a worldwide basis, but is committed to community service and fellowship locally as well. Rotarians follow a clear and concise code of ethics that consists of four questions about anything the club or its members may say or do:

1. Is it the TRUTH?
2. Is it FAIR to all concerned?
3. Will it build GOODWILL and BETTER FRIENDSHIPS?
4. Will it be BENEFICIAL to all concerned?

Every Rotary club in the world holds itself to these values and aligns its actions accordingly.

Let's go back to the world of science. Remember how the intention of the observer affects the behavior of the subatomic particle? If we expect it, it'll happen. If we carry with us an attitude of emergency, our world will be urgent. If we carry with us an attitude of insufficiency, our world will be skimpy. Living with a negative bias – expecting the worst – can become a self-fulfilling prophecy. But if we carry with us an attitude of gratitude, our world will be one of blessings. It's pretty simple – but it isn't easy.

Seeking first the Kingdom of God means we have to align ourselves with our highest understanding of God in everything we think, say and do. Our highest understanding of God is continuously evolving as a result of our living in the world and experiencing the back-and-forth of pain and pleasure, joy and sorrow, work and play, day and night. Every time we pause and withdraw into the quiet of prayer or meditation, contemplation or inspiration, we are realigned with our inner divinity, and we understand ourselves and our worlds a little bit more.

We bring our perceptions back to spirit and examine our reactions, testing to see if we could have been more loving, patient, brave, helpful or generous. In humility we ask the most secret part of our hearts what we could have done better, and we let the reassurance of Divine Love and Understanding wash over us.

We continuously align ourselves with our highest understanding of God by keeping an eye on ourselves, checking to be sure that our thoughts, words and actions reflect who we really are in Spirit. Those times in the quiet are the soil in which the seeds of understanding are planted, to sprout and bloom into habitual behavior that is fully aligned with our highest understanding of God.

What are you aligned with? What are your values? Does your life reflect the values you hold most dear? What about your work and play? Are you investing your creative energy in seeking the

Kingdom of God, whatever that might look like for you? Are you doing your job in the Divine Ecosystem, using the gifts and talents that were hardwired and pre-programmed into you? Beloved, are you not of more value than the lilies of the field?

Of course you are, and your gifts and talents are of vital importance to our world. You grow and are clothed in glory greater than Solomon's by living your dreams and desires and overcoming your obstacles and adversities.

The seeds of Spirit take root in the
undisturbed silence of meditation.

They are watered and warmed by Divine Love,
and they bloom and bear fruit as I fulfill my life's purpose.

Chapter 5
Everyday Spirituality

You are the light of the world. A city built on a hill cannot be hidden. No one after lighting a lamp puts it under the bushel basket, but on the lampstand, and it gives light to all in the house. In the same way, let your light shine before others, so that they may see your good works and give glory to your Father in heaven. Matt. 5:14-16

Every day, my spirit lights my lamp.
As I bear the light of my lamp, I light the world with the glory of God.

Nesting dolls are a folk art tradition from Russia. Meticulously carved and colorfully painted, the outer doll comes apart to reveal a similar, smaller doll inside. The inner doll opens to reveal an even smaller version of the same doll, which also opens to reveal the tiniest doll of all. Think about the last time you were in a public place, perhaps a restaurant or a shop. You may have seen people you didn't know – and you might have noticed their size, shape, outfit or gestures. You didn't know their names or anything about them other than what you observed from afar. That's like the outer doll.

But suppose that you were seated next to a stranger in the customer waiting area at the auto mechanic's garage. You might strike up a casual conversation and discover something about that person's occupation, hobby or family in addition to noticing their outer appearance. You've opened up the outer doll and are now seeing the next smaller one.

If you were to serve on a committee with a stranger, in time you might come to know more about them. Perhaps you would get a sense of what they value, what they love, what they fear, what they wish for. You've removed the second doll and are holding the third.

But then one day in your growing intimacy with this person, a crisis erupts, and you experience the depth of their character and the strength of their spiritual connection in a way you hadn't imagined. You've seen the tiny inner doll, and that's the pure, original, straight-from-God self.

The innermost self, the secret place of the most high, the heart of hearts where the individual consciousness emerges from God consciousness – all these are attempts to describe who we really are in the deepest truth of our beings. That self is pure energy, pure intelligence, pure love and pure life, an expression of God through the mind and body of one individual.

Everyday spirituality is the moment-to-moment sense of self as a spiritual being, first and foremost. It means that thoughts, words and deeds arise from that innermost place, the place where human consciousness emerges from God consciousness. It requires knowing oneself as a spiritual being having a human experience, rather than the other way around: a human being having the occasional spiritual experience. Your spiritual identity shines through your outer layers, the increasingly larger outer dolls, with greater brilliance and clarity as you claim and inhabit more fully your legacy as an expression of God. Imagine that with every awakening in your consciousness, your outer layers become clearer, purer, more polished and brilliant like the lantern of a lighthouse on a rocky shore. Your inner light is a beacon, and you never know when its clarity will be the life-saving signal for a stranger in the fog!

Trinities

Trinities abound in our culture. There's something very satisfying about a threesome – it's a handy structure for organizing ideas. Stories usually have a beginning, a middle and an end. A popular model for curriculum development used to include a pretest, instruction and a post-test. The red triangle logo of the Young Men's Christian Association is a familiar trinity. The design was proposed in 1891 by Dr. Lester Gulick as the symbol for the YMCA with the equal sides of the triangle standing for "man's essential unity: body, mind and spirit . . ."

The Holy Trinity is a traditional Christian concept of God in three persons: God the Father, Christ the Son and the Holy Ghost. They're all God, but the Father, Son and Holy Ghost or Holy Spirit represent different aspects or activities of God.

Another trinity is the metaphysical trinity of Mind, Idea and Expression. God is the Mind, which does the thinking and is active in humans as the Spirit. The Christ is the Idea brought into being by the Mind and is active in humans as the soul, or the heart/mind. The Expression is the manifestation of the Idea in the world, active in humans as the body. Thus, we have another trinity in three phases of man: Spirit, Soul and Body.

In the late 1800s, Sigmund Freud identified three parts of the self, or psyche. He called them the *id*, the *ego* and the *super ego*. He said that the *id* was the part of the mind that acted on input from the senses, unconscious and based on survival and pleasure. He explained the *ego* as the self-aware part of the mind that functioned in communication with the outer world. He described the *super ego* as the higher mind concerned with right and wrong and saw the *ego* or self-aware mind as being the mediator in the conflict between the *id* and the *super ego.*

A spiritual view of the mind modifies the Freudian structure by describing the *subconscious* as the part of the mind that stores information for later reference. The *conscious* mind is the part that interacts with the outer world, receiving impressions and information from the subconscious as well as new input from the environment. The *superconscious* is the God-mind, from which Divine inspiration is drawn. The individual can direct the conscious mind to act on input from the subconscious or the superconscious.

The fully realized spiritual being is the holy union of all three of the Freudian parts of the psyche with the metaphysical structure of Mind/Idea/Expression and the spirit/soul/body of the phases of man embraced in wholeness as the human being. The physical body, expressing itself through the subconscious *id*, and the rational/emotional soul, expressing itself as the conscious *ego*, are integral components of the spiritual being having a human experience. The spirit, expressing itself through the *super ego* as the superconscious, is the Divine. It is the individualization of God, the Creator. In order to live on the earth and enjoy the human experience, the spiritual being requires a physical body, which includes a brain, and a rational being, which includes the mind and the emotions. The whole package of *id, ego* and *super ego*, or body, soul and spirit, is the self.

You were a holy spiritual being before your conception because your spirit was in God, in the divine oneness from which all souls emerge. Conception was the beginning of your physical being, the manifestation of divine life in the mass of cells that grew into your body. At birth your body emerged and was separated from that of your mother, a complete and viable vessel for your unique and holy spiritual self. Being separated from your mother's womb was pretty scary and uncomfortable, but you were still whole and perfect in every way as a human expression of God. You had to emerge in order to continue to grow "in wisdom and in stature" (Luke 2:52, NRSV). Your growth and development continued throughout your childhood while you "lived so successfully disguised to (yourself) as a child." (James Agee, *Knoxville*). Your spiritual being has always been, is now and forever will be whole, perfect and complete. It's just the physical/mental/emotional self that is learning and growing.

Any sense of loss or separation from God is an illusion, generated by your acceptance of and belief in your physical and emotional experiences. As long as you are living, you are a holy expression of the life of God in every cell of your body. Every human is entitled to live as a spiritual being, free of what might be called human limitation. How did we lose sight of ourselves?

Spirituality is an integral component of humanity. We are born pure, worthy and imbued with holiness. As we travel the path of growth and maturity, our teeth come in and then fall out to be replaced by bigger, stronger teeth. Our brains build dense tangles of neurons, only to be refined into functional neural networks by our experiences and activity. Our motor skills and our understanding of gravity grow and are refined by our increasingly accurate ability to knock things down, pick them up and manipulate them.

Just so, our experience and expression of our innate spirituality evolves through our interaction with our inner worlds and our outer worlds. The baby's brain processes this brave new world in growing complexity and subtlety. At first a newborn's perceptions are of warmth, safety, food, nurturing and so on. As time goes on and the brain develops, the child learns to identify, think, respond, choose, reject and interact with the environment. The joyous enthusiasm of the infant is tempered by the bumps and bruises of childhood, and its buoyant self-expression as a spiritual being is occasionally dimmed by disappointments, but the inner light of spirit glows ever brighter as the child learns and grows to adulthood. As with any other life skill, everyday spirituality grows stronger with dedicated practice.

In everyday spirituality we are flexible and adaptable. We rise to any occasion with creativity, courage, healing, regeneration, grace and joy. Humanity has survived eons of catastrophes, natural as well as man-made, because of the flexible, creative spirit that created humanity and the natural world in which humanity lives.

When we practice everyday spirituality, we are conscious and aware. We consciously choose to express spirit and are fearless and self-assured. Each moment, we draw thought, choice and breath from God, the one source. We follow the purest and truest way, always choosing the highest and best for all concerned, and are committed to bringing the serenity and centeredness of communion with spirit into expression in the outer world.

Living everyday spirituality, we ride the crest of existence confidently and serenely, knowing that there is no point naming ideas, events or actions good or bad. What might be perceived as a "bad" thing may actually be a blessing as it generates a reaction that creates something new that is perceived as good. What might be perceived as a "good" thing might actually turn out to be a "bad" thing as it leads to overindulgence or exhaustion. We are delightful and charming, loving ourselves in our fullness and loving the world in its infinite variety. Everyday spirituality is a powerful model of consistency, eternally new and fresh with the creative energy of spirit, and unchanging in its intensity and power.

Escaping the Karmic Soup

Karma is a term from the Hindu tradition that refers to the influence of one's actions in the current lifetime and the consequences of those actions in subsequent lifetimes. It's the energy that causes your good actions in this life to result in blessings in your next life and creates the unfortunate circumstances in this life as a result of wrongdoing in a previous life. The "karmic wheel" refers to the cycle of birth, life and death in which rebirth begins the next revolution of the wheel.

As we live our lives, we develop an accumulation of attitudes and expectations based on our prior experiences. Whether we believe in reincarnation or not, we live immersed in this accumulation, or "karmic soup," of ideas and energies. In this karmic soup, we respond to new experiences with the same comfortable, habitual behaviors and interpretations that have gotten us thus far in our lives. So how do we climb out of this accumulation, this soup of circumstances and situations?

You may have heard the expression, "Christ is Lord of Karma." Jesus the Christ embodied the perfect Oneness with God that clears and heals any kind of karmic connection. Knowing and practicing our conscious connection with God opens the floodgates of healing, harmonizing energy that wash away the effects of limited understanding and misguided action. We can always, at any time, choose to fully inhabit and express our highest and best selves. Discovering, protecting and preserving the sense of spirituality in the self begin with coaching and teaching by wise and loving parents during childhood, then continue with dedicated spiritual hygiene thereafter. Regardless of early experiences, dedicated spiritual hygiene can repair, restore and strengthen the sense of oneness with God. Spiritual hygiene means prayer, meditation, contemplation, introspection and service to God in humankind. Building the strength of self to withstand hurts, disappointments and criticisms is a lifelong project. The potential for growth, awareness and wholeness is limited only by the willingness, or unwillingness, to get up and try again.

Christian tradition teaches that the path to redemption and salvation is repentance. The root of the word "repent" bears no resemblance to the English word, but is an ancient Greek word "*metanoia*," or rethinking. The writers of the New Testament wrote in Greek in which there was only one very specific meaning for any given word. "*Meta*" means beyond or after. "*Noia*" means perception, understanding or mind. At the time the New Testament was written, the meaning of "*metanoia*" was reorientation or changing one's mind. It came to imply a new awareness of having been estranged from one's deity and later to mean the acknowledgement of one's mistakes or sins.

Unfortunately, the scholars who translated it into English centuries later assumed that *metanoia*, or "rethinking," meant to regret or be sorry for something, which was definitely not the original meaning. So the path to redemption and salvation is rethinking – changing one's mind – not repenting or being sorry for our actions. If we change our mind, we think differently, and we interact with our worlds differently. We understand circumstances from a different vantage point, seeing things that we missed before and noticing connections and relationships that had escaped us.

Repentance and asking forgiveness are often partners in the quest for redemption and salvation. But remember, God does not judge. God loves us unconditionally and accepts our missteps as Mom accepts the spilled milk of the 2-year-old. The 2- year-old didn't quite understand that the milk bottle was heavy and slippery but has more information as a result of the experience – metanoia. Repentance, or rethinking, and then asking forgiveness merely indicate our wish to return to grace, which is our normal state. And we were never out of grace – we just thought we were.

Consider the Garden of Eden story. Adam and Eve were frolicking in Paradise, naming all the bunnies, doves and earthworms, eating whatever they desired from any plant in the garden – except one. God had warned Adam not to eat of the Tree of the Knowledge of Good and Evil. Now, God had a perfectly reasonable motive for this. As long as Adam didn't know the difference between good and evil, he lived in a world that met his every need. He had nothing to worry about, all his needs were met, and all he had to do was keep God company. Adam may have thought, "It's all good."

But that nasty serpent talked Eve into eating that apple, then she talked Adam into having just one little bite and boom – big trouble for the man and woman. Cast out of Paradise, doomed to earn their food by the sweat of their brows. Not only that, but Eve was condemned to suffer pangs during childbirth, probably because she started the whole mess by listening to the serpent. All of a sudden, Adam and Eve had a very clear understanding of the difference between good and evil. And to this day, so do we.

Do you think God knows good and evil? Or does God just know it all as it is? In the creation story, God calls it good. You see, when we name something good, that's what it is for us. When we name something bad, that's what it is for us. But if we can stretch our minds enough to entertain the possibility that some good might emerge from something that looks really bad, we leave the door open for things to work out on their own without circumstances having to overcome our expectations of disaster. Or maybe, with the door open, a whole new understanding can come in and change our view of the whole situation!

A traditional interpretation of the Adam and Eve story emphasizes the disobedience and "original sin" aspects of the story, but let's look at it another way. God, as the loving Parent, wished to protect His progeny from the pain of knowing good and evil, so God forbade Adam and Eve to eat from that one particular tree. As most parents discover, forbidding something is often a good way to guarantee that the offspring will try it – soon. Being created in the image and likeness of God and knowing good and evil freed Adam and Eve to emulate their Creator fully – and we as their descendants have been exploring that freedom ever since.

It's awfully difficult to live in this physical world with the complexities we've created for ourselves and the differences of viewpoint that we've invented. We've made the human existence a physical challenge – much more complex than whether to eat the fruit of that one particular tree or be content with the abundance from all the other trees. But the solution is still the same – rethinking and reconnecting and going back into the world with renewed clarity and sanctity.

"Breaking the karmic wheel" is another way of describing the concept of grace – the eternal healing power of Divine Life and the unearned blessing of God's infinite and unconditional love for God's Creation. Just as the hiker relies on a stout walking stick to support her through rough places on the trail, metanoia is the hiking staff that supports us as we walk the path of everyday spirituality. Few individuals have experienced continuous everyday spirituality during a lifetime. Jesus was one; Mohammed, Gautama the Buddha, Lao-Tzu and Mother Teresa were others. There probably have been many more, but we don't have an adequate reporting system in place yet.

Most of us begin our lives unaware of the infinite possibilities within, and we accept erroneous information from the outer world that convinces us we are imperfect, flawed and incomplete. As in the Garden of Eden story, we begin life in the paradise of infancy, knowing ourselves as nothing but whole, perfect and beloved. Then we realize our separate identities, and the knowledge of good and evil changes the rules. We find ourselves outside paradise trying to figure out how to live and take care of ourselves. When we rethink and return to knowing our infinite and eternal heritage as children of God, we are once again in communion with wholeness and perfection. The only difference is that now we know it, and we are responsible for the results of our actions and our choices. If we make decisions and act based on appearance rather than Truth, then the first thing we know, we're back in the karmic soup, at the mercies of the vagaries of our outer worlds.

So how do we get out of there? How do we get from our everyday selves to our spiritual selves without a bolt of lightning or a magic spell to jolt us over? One step at a time. One choice at a time. One thought at a time. Lovingly examining every thought, choice and step to check for Godliness. Self-knowledge is a precious commodity gained by diligent effort and sometimes painful reflection.

Meditation and Metanoia

Let's go back to the story of Adam and Eve being tossed out of the garden. They ate of the Tree of the Knowledge of Good and Evil – they all of a sudden "knew" there was good and bad. As long as they didn't know that, they were safe, happy and secure in there. But once they were aware of the possibility of something other than good, *pffft*, there goes the Garden! So ever since, humanity has been trying to heal that breach and find its way back to Oneness, back to the single-minded consciousness of God as all-good, all-loving and all-One.

Joseph, of many-colored coat fame, is a great example of metanoia. Many years after they had betrayed him, he explained to his brothers, "You meant evil against me, but God meant it for good." Joseph had a deep connection with God, built over a lifetime of dedicated prayer and meditation. Rethinking his circumstances, framing them in the light of God's infinite love for each of His children, allowed him to release and rise above the hurt and anger of unfair treatment. He was free to follow the path of Divine Guidance, growing through the years of limitation and hardship to abundant prosperity and honor. If we apply a metaphysical interpretation, his story might be a metaphor in which the brothers are our ordinary, normal human thoughts of having been mistreated and abused, and Joseph's enlightened prayer consciousness is the spiritual self which can make even the worst circumstances into blessings.

Living as one's spiritual self is the result of conscious choices on a daily, moment-to-moment basis over many years in the world. Sometimes we show up as our spiritual self for a brief shining moment but then our light is obscured by clouds of judgment, doubt, fear or habit. The surest way to touch and bring forth one's spiritual self is dedicated meditation and vigilant metanoia. Vigilance means to watch – keep an eye out for, be on guard for. Metanoia, or re-thinking, is like grooming our thoughts by observing, choosing, cleansing, changing or releasing them. Vigilance in grooming our thoughts will gradually but ultimately bring about that transformation from fear or confusion to Sanctity. The builder of Sanctity will be ever more vigilant as he grows in clarity, and his discernment is refined, noticing increasingly subtle distinctions in thoughts and feelings.

Sitting with quiet expectancy in deep inner Silence reconnects us with Universal Mind, the Mind beyond our conscious mind that is the infinite Source of more than we can ever conceive. Time in Nature, joyous time with loved ones and excellent music, art or literature are all reminders of what it feels like to live as one's spiritual self. The inner question, "but what if there was another point of view?" can help us rise out of our habitual responses into a more loving, compassionate, courageous view of the situation.

As we move through life experiences and make choices, our repeated observations, perceptions and interpretations shape our ability to live as our highest, purest Self. God, "I AM who I AM," the Universal Source of Being, is infinite. Interactions with Being are infinite, especially as we build our connection with the infinite through our practice of meditation. We experience meditation when we quiet our minds and enter the inner Silence. Interactions with the infinite Being are possible only when we listen intently without commenting. The discipline of following deep inner silence is the key to the profound revelations of meditation because it is in that sacred silence that our minds expand to contemplate the infinity of Being. The time we spend in communion with God strengthens the magnetic power in our spiritual compasses as we refine our sanctity. Vigilant metanoia builds constructive, flexible habits of thought, and dedicated meditation opens the door to oneness so that we become more sensitive to being out of communion with our source.

Living as one's spiritual self means that one is as fully Godlike as possible – being loving, generous, gentle, confident, joyous, creative, powerful, whatever attributes feel most holy and pure. The hard part is remembering to be in one's spiritual self when the outer world intrudes with challenges, obstacles, discord or conflict. The HeartMath tools of FreezeFrame and Heart Lock-In are powerful techniques for stopping that nosedive of despair when feeling overwhelmed. Then the metanoia hiking staff, re-thinking, helps us remember to stop and consider the power of grace, love, generosity and patience.

Of course, we know that life and limb are to be preserved and protected; most of us are not quite ready to accept bodily harm to ourselves or loved ones in the name of achieving sanctity. But in those smaller day-to-day choices, when perhaps the stakes aren't quite so high, perhaps we could pause to choose a Godly course of thought or action rather than a habitual or unconsidered one.

Deconstruction

Have you ever had this conversation with yourself?

I'm <u>cranky!</u>
> (Do I need to pray/meditate?)

Heck, no – it'll only make me have to be more Godlike. I'd rather be cranky. Then I get to be <u>right</u>.
> (Whose voice was that?
> Uh-oh – here comes another growth spurt!)

"Out there" needs to change. Somebody else is making my world all wrong. It's not my fault. No wonder I can't . . . haven't . . . didn't . . .

Maybe you don't get cranky – but you've probably had the experience of feeling that the world was simply <u>wrong.</u>

One of the most difficult pieces of living as the spiritual self is accepting the pain and suffering of deconstruction. The Hindu deity Shiva is the god of destruction, and his role is vitally important in the balance of the universe. Can you imagine our world if nothing ever decayed or broke down? We've already considered the importance of biological recycling – composting – and made peace with that idea. We've looked at the process of shaping and pruning and choosing this or not this and accepted that process as a part of being alive. But we aren't always in charge of the shaping, pruning and choosing – sometimes it's initiated by forces beyond our control.

So what if, instead of being all wrong, it's already all fine, and we can make it better? What if all the resources we need are already there, with all the energy and matter and potential, and all we have to do is <u>create</u>? All we have to do is be God – the original creative force, the only creative force – active in our bodies, with our minds, in our spheres of experience? Then the deconstruction becomes just another obstacle or adversity to be overcome or "grown through" by the creative Spirit of the Individual.

God didn't blame or criticize. God said, "let there be . . ." and there was . . . , and God called it good.

God didn't whine or make excuses. God didn't procrastinate or create a task force or appoint a committee. Or get up a petition or launch a marketing survey. God said, "let there be . . ." and there was . . . , and God saw that it was good.

In the face of deconstruction, whether by natural forces such as an earthquake or hurricane, or human forces such as accident, illness or violence, your spiritual self stands tall in its infinite wisdom and creativity. Grief and anger are common human responses to pain and fear. Acting out of grief and anger can be devastatingly damaging and destructive or magnificently creative and constructive. The intensity of the grief and anger is directly related to the depth of the love and compassion in the heart of the spiritual self, and the creative and constructive energy available is proportional to the depth of the commitment to spirit, life and love.

Jesus cleansed the Temple of the money-changers with a great outburst of energy. The money-changers probably saw it as destructive anger, but we are told that Jesus acted in defense of the Holy Temple of God. He acted with love and with power. Loving power – energy expended in integrity with our highest understanding of divine love and life – is our best resource for making things right when they appear to have gone wrong.

Maintaining and nurturing our spiritual connection through prayerful meditation and metanoia are vital to staying poised and centered in the face of challenging experiences. If we are "prayed up," filled with and attuned to our Source, we can act confidently and with assurance of the highest and best results. Our creative energy, coupled with our devotion to Spirit, calls forth the grace and healing we seek.

Rather than seeing the devastation and wreckage of deconstruction, the spiritual self sees the opportunity and potential for healing, growth and fulfillment. Vigilant metanoia and dedicated meditation are the keys to sanctifying the self. We may have inherited the knowledge of good and evil as a result of our forebears' disobedience, but we have also inherited the Kingdom of God. All we have to do is call it good and keep on keeping on.

Our spiritual selves are a work in progress, one which adapts to stimuli creatively, constructively, productively. Each spiritual self exists in a state of joy and grace, abundance and peace – regardless of outer circumstances. It is the individuality, the God-Self, conscious and aware. It is spirit individualized and the origin of the holy individual. The spiritual self chooses consciously to express Spirit fearlessly and with complete assurance. Each moment, every thought, choice and breath are drawn from the One Source. The spiritual self always chooses the purest, truest way, always the highest and best for all concerned. The spiritual self brings the serenity and centeredness of meditation into expression in the outer world.

With every breath, I AM who I AM:
Pure, Holy, Spiritual.

Chapter 6: Epilogue
How Does the World Work, and How Do I Fit In?

Then God said, 'Let us make humankind in our image, according to our likeness; and let them have dominion over the fish of the sea, and over the birds of the air, and over the cattle, and over all the wild animals of the earth, and over every creeping thing that creeps upon the earth.' Gen 1:26

As God's likeness, I accept the sacred trust
of dominion over my world.

So again Jesus said to them, ". . . I came that they may have life, and have it abundantly." John 10:10

I am here to give, to serve and to love.

The world works according to laws of nature such as give and take, ebb and flow, rain and sun, day and night. We live in the natural world and, as thinking beings, have come up with all kinds of cosmologies about how it works and why it works that way. Humankind has put a lot of energy into making itself comfortable in the world, fitting in with more or less success depending on your point of view.

The natural world in which we live is a wondrous place. Planet Earth is an exquisite home, full of variety and contrast and beauty and simplicity. Even the atmosphere is an invisible miracle – we can walk outside and take a deep, refreshing breath, knowing there's plenty of air to go around. We let go of our deep breath, blowing out all the waste gases our bodies can't use, and the plants thank us for the carbon dioxide. In return they give off fresh oxygen for us to breathe in next time. Everything Mother Nature put on our planet serves and is served by something else She put on the planet. As with all siblings, there is occasionally a bit of rivalry for the resources of the Mother, but we get along pretty well for the most part, and we're learning to do better.

Cosmology

Webster defines cosmology as "a branch of metaphysics that deals with the universe as an orderly system." Although the science of cosmology deals with questions about the origins of the universe, our use of the term refers to our personal spheres of experience and influence.

Each of us lives in a world of home and family, occupation and recreation, supply and demand, waking and sleeping, solitude and togetherness. We've navigated our lives and our worlds fairly successfully up till now and have formulated a set of expectations to explain how the world works. The interesting part is that your world works exactly the way you think it does.

As we navigate our daily lives, we act on prior information and experience, and we expect results and reactions similar to those we've gotten before. We've built our own "cosmologies" – personal explanations of how the world works – and tested them for a lifetime, adapting and adjusting them as events and circumstances dictate. Every so often, our cosmologies get shaken up by a major event, and we have to revise or remodel them to suit our new circumstances. Then we shift into a new rhythm of life and continue on our path, revised edition of the cosmology firmly in place to guide and support our daily living.

Common elements of cosmologies have to do with deities, morals, values, ethics, hygiene, consequences, expectations and lifestyle. We adopt elements of our families' cosmologies in constructing our own, and we have a pretty complete one in place by age seven. The cosmology grows in complexity and scope through the teen years and early adulthood and by the mid-twenties is well established. We gravitate towards those whose cosmologies are compatible with our own, though we may enjoy stimulating conversations with those holding contrasting views.

Even as adults, our cosmologies may be challenged by events and circumstances. Marrying into a family of a different culture, moving to a new part of the world, even completing a college degree or other educational goal can affect our personal cosmology. But we work it out and come to a new level of stasis or comfort with our newly revised version of our cosmology.

Physicists have shown that thoughts, feelings and intentions influence the behavior of subatomic particles. Subatomic particles are the building blocks of matter, but sometimes they show up as waves of energy instead. So thoughts, feelings and intentions can influence the movement of energy. It may be a bit of a stretch, but it's possible that our thoughts, feelings and intentions can influence matter and energy.

Our cosmologies work because of the thoughts and feelings that constructed them and also because our worlds are built from matter and energy, which are influenced by thoughts and feelings. Our thoughts and feelings are affected by our contact with matter and energy, and the circle continues. We interact with our worlds and are acted upon by our perceptions of our world. We custom-design our worlds to fit who we are and what we need – and we create ourselves anew to fit the worlds we inhabit.

Mind the Gap

Travelers on the London Underground are reminded to "Mind the Gap" – look out for the space between the station platform and the floor of the subway car as they step through the door. Medical insurers provide "gap insurance" – a policy providing coverage in case there are expenses not covered by primary or secondary insurance providers. Gaps can be tricky, especially if you don't know they're there.

The "is-ought gap" is one that sometimes shows up in a cosmology. It's the distance between what is (actual conditions) and what ought to be (our conclusions). We assume that our cosmology, our world-view, is smoothly intact and seamless until we encounter a situation in which doing what we have always done doesn't get us what we've always gotten. An example of the "is-ought gap" in a cosmology might be the rude awakening of discovering that a check you deposited didn't get posted in time to cover the check you wrote to pay a bill. Depositing a good check ought to mean the funds are available, but the fact is that the bank put a hold on it because it was drawn on an out-of-town bank. So your cosmology got a revision, reminding you to next time make sure the deposit has been posted before you write a check against it.

On a more subtle level, our brains are designed to look for what's out there, not for what's missing. If we are looking for evidence to support a conclusion we've drawn, we may not perceive evidence that contradicts it. If we don't discover evidence that supports the conclusion, our brains create a story to explain it. Once we've created our story, we act as if it is true and then construe any new evidence as support for our original conclusion. This new story becomes the gap in our cosmology – the point at which our version of how the world works breaks down.

In her book *Mastering Life's Energies*, Dr. Maria Nemeth uses her "Four-Box Model" to illustrate how we navigate our gaps. She begins with a conclusion, which is an assessment of a situation that we have accepted as true. The second box is the evidence that our assessment or conclusion is indeed true, regardless of whether we actually found the evidence or made some up. The third box is how we act based on our evidence, what we say or do because we're convinced of the conclusion. The fourth box is how others respond to our actions and words, which have been derived from our conclusion.

When we notice others responding to our behavior that was based on our commitment to our first conclusion, our interpretation of their responses will continue to support our conclusion unless we have learned some ways to choose more interesting or rewarding thoughts or conclusions. Over the years, Dr. Nemeth has coached thousands of clients through the process of dismantling their "systems of knowing," how they gather evidence and draw conclusions. She has helped people around the world live more productive, luminous lives as they navigate their cosmologies and their gaps with clarity, focus, ease and grace.

Our responses to our "is-ought gaps" are great barometers of how effective our cosmologies are in telling us how the world works, and they give us useful feedback on how we're fitting into the world.

The Perfect Fit

Have you ever walked into a brand new situation and immediately felt at home? Or perhaps completely out of place? Your cosmology probably had some influence on either situation and gave you some guidance about how to proceed. When we feel at home, we may feel like reaching out to others and connecting with new kindred spirits – or we may prefer to bask in the comfort of safety and solitude. Feeling out of place might prompt us to step into our extroverted mode, reaching out to connect with others in search of a kindred spirit, or we might step back to observe and notice our surroundings in an effort to understand how to assimilate more easily.

Fitting into the world is a quest that begins in toddlerhood, just as understanding how the world works becomes a fascination. A 2-year-old really needs to know that he has the power to build a stack of blocks and demolish it with one gleeful swipe. Lots of lessons are being learned about balance, structure, scale, force and gravity. Fitting into the family structure begins at birth and continues with accepting Mom and Dad as the authorities in the family. Fitting in with others isn't really on the developmental radar until age 4 or 5, when friendship and sharing become very important. Fitting into the classroom or family by understanding and respecting rules is of paramount importance to a 7-year-old, but in adolescence, when self-expression and meaningful work become top priorities in daily living, fitting in means debating and revising the rules.

We have learned about fitting in – fulfilling the expectations of employers, partners, associates – and about moving on when we couldn't or wouldn't fit in any more. We have learned about compromising in order to fit in, either by changing our expectations or our actions. We have experienced circumstances in which we felt ourselves blossom – where we felt honored, appreciated, challenged and accepted – and other circumstances in which we felt ourselves wither, feeling ourselves alienated, criticized or hopelessly wrong.

Fitting in means that we understand how our world works and that we feel confident of our ability to navigate and negotiate events and circumstances successfully. It means that we feel valued and significant and that we value our significant others as well. Fitting in means that we have a place in our world, a place defined by our roles and relationships, our functions and experiences. When we don't fit in, we seek to fit in elsewhere or to make adjustments so that we will fit better.

Fitting in is an exchange of love, a function of connection and communication. It's a matter of doing and interacting, giving input to and receiving feedback from others in our world. Fitting in is a form of success, feeling that our presence or activity has benefitted or enhanced some aspect of the world. If we raise the most exquisite rose ever seen, we can enjoy it in solitude and know that we fit in with nature and our garden, or we can share it with others and enjoy their appreciation of its beauty and fragrance as they enjoy the rose. Fitting in is important because it means there's a place of belonging, a place of acceptance. It might also mean there's a reason to be there, a function, a relationship.

Fitting in means that you have something to give that is needed by someone else. The things you're good at are blessings to those around you, and others around you have talents and gifts that are blessings to you. Fitting in is satisfying, affirming, productive, harmonious and subjective. A guest at a party may find another guest obtrusive and out-of-place, but a third guest might relish the quirky humor he displayed. Fitting in – more than an absolute yes-or-no judgment – may be a matter of personal preference and perhaps even a matter of compatible cosmologies. Fitting in is an experience of mutual flow, as in the conversation that lasted well into the wee hours to your very great surprise.

The world works on action and reaction, ebb and flow, give and take, motion and stillness. Regardless of the path we choose, our action (or inaction) in the world generates a response. We create the space where we fit into the world by our attitudes, our actions, our expectations and our choices.

God with Skin on

Regardless of your cosmology and how you fit in, you're still God in a skin suit. You are the embodiment of a divine idea, a spiritual being having a human experience. You may have your human limitations – can't help it, it comes with the skin suit – but you are an infinite, eternal Spirit that is infallible. So no matter what your cosmology says, or how you feel you fit in the world, sanctifying your Self has one purpose.

The purpose of sanctifying your Self is the fuller expression of God through the unique talents and abilities that are hardwired into your physical body and brain and are programmed into your mind and heart. Biology is responsible for the hardwiring; life experience develops the programming. To express God is to live in as God-like a manner as possible – to be Godly in the highest sense of the word. To be Godly is to live as love, joy, health, courage, growth, strength, power; to be fearless, compassionate, confident, effective, serene and eternal. This is a very large package of very great ideas.

This large package applies to all humanity, regardless of race, creed or culture. God created us in God's image, after God's likeness, and gave us dominion over all the earth. This is huge – dominion means lordship. A lord is one who is in charge of the realm, the kingdom, a large geographic area. Remember the parable where Jesus said, "From everyone to whom much has been given, much will be required; and from the one to whom much has been entrusted, even more will be demanded,"? Having dominion, being in charge of the realm is a big deal – an enormous responsibility.

We human beings have enormous resources and enormous responsibilities. We are the stewards of our own consciousnesses and of the world. The planet and all its inhabitants. And then, Jesus said that He came that they may have life and have it abundantly. He had already told us that the things He did we would do also – does that mean that we are here to help them have life abundantly? Who are "they," anyway?

Marianne Williamson, in her book *Return to Love*, writes:

> Our deepest fear is not that we are inadequate. Our deepest fear is that we are powerful beyond measure. It is our light, not our darkness that most frightens us. We ask ourselves, 'Who am I to be brilliant, gorgeous, talented, fabulous?' Actually, who are you not to be? You are a child of God. Your playing small does not serve the world.

"They" are all those in your world who see you, hear you, know of you, pass you on the street, sell you your groceries or sit behind you at the movies. They are counting on you to be brilliant, gorgeous, talented, fabulous, prosperous, healthy and sublimely happy because when they see you doing it, at some level they know they can do it too.

When you live your life to the fullest extent allowable by law (Divine law, of course), you raise the bar for all the rest of us. When you live and love with every ounce of your being, you send out radiant energy that says "yes, you can!" to the rest of us. If you decide that the best way to be God-in-your-skin-suit is to set a new record for swimming the English Channel, you will use every talent, ability, experience and resource to make that happen. By doing so, you will attract and empower all the support teams and coaches who help you directly, the cheering squads who believe in you and cheer you on and the rest of the world who will be touched in some way by your effort and energy.

In the Prologue of this book, we began our work by wondering "who am I, and how did I get here?" We considered the possibility that we are spirit in a body, having a human experience, coming up to the present moment as the summation of our experiences. We have explored numerous communities, environments and occupations, finding various degrees of satisfaction, frustration, accomplishment and defeat. Now, we finally consider the rest of the question: "How does the world work, and how do I fit in?"

Somehow, your life purpose is to serve the world. Just as the lilies serve by holding the hillsides in place, your service will be as unique and original as you are because you're the only you there has ever been or will ever be. The highest and best gift of the spiritual self is service. The highest and best that any spiritual being can achieve is to envelop all creation in that unconditional love and light that empowers the self of another. Somehow, fulfilling the divine potential within yourself and serving the divine in all creation is the path to perfect expression of your spiritual self.

In Judaism, an act of loving kindness is generally called a *mitzvah*. The Christian tradition urges charity, which is giving to those in need. In the Hindu tradition, the word *seva* (SAYvuh) means service in the highest and best possible meaning of the word. All three traditions, and countless others around the world, emphasize service with no thought of return, no thought of acknowledgement. Sacred service means doing whatever you can to make the world a little better than it was – not out of a sense of obligation but out of a sense of oneness. Sacred service is given from a full heart and a strong soul. It is a gift shared out of abundance and love – as God gives. If you can adopt a day-in-day-out attitude of service, you will be amazed at the sense of personal power and deep gratitude that begins to permeate your being. You will be fulfilling your true identity as a child of God, created in the image and likeness of God.

Sacred service does not judge. It does not decide who is or isn't worthy to receive its ministrations. It is unconditional – given as it is needed, without qualification. The generosity of sacred service is something akin to the graciousness of the ideal host, who is delighted to have the opportunity to make his guests happy.

An attitude of sacred service shifts your sensitivity from one of self-centered rigidity to one of other-centered flexibility. Seeing your world and companions through the eyes of sacred service allows you to see as God sees with the infinite confidence of an all-powerful being of light. Living in sacred service puts you in the energy of affirmation, accepting and living in your own unique and precious Individuality.

How better to affirm your oneness with the creative power of the universe than to find a way to serve? Not just any way, but <u>your</u> way of using the talents and abilities that were hardwired into your being at birth and the skills and knowledge that have been programmed into you by your life experiences. Being your spiritual self means leaving things nicer than they were when you got there.

The important thing to remember is that no matter what your past has been, you can always, at any time, choose to fully inhabit and express your most spiritual self. As you move through your life's experiences and make life choices, your repeated observations, perceptions and interpretations shape your expression of the Divine. Every time you expand your awareness of your sanctity, the world breathes a little easier. God said, "Let there be you!" – and there was your spiritual self, and God saw it and called it good. Amen.

Sanctified by God in me, as me, through me,
I am integral and indispensable to my world.

Conclusion

*Now if you are unwilling to serve the L*ORD*, choose this day whom you will serve . . . but as for me and my household, we will serve the L*ORD*.* Joshua 24:15

This day, and every day, I serve my highest understanding of God.

So when you feel scared or worried or envious or irritated, which God are you serving? Are you serving the Lord, or the visible world, or what you've heard others say? Are you buying into the notion that you are a limited being with finite resources of life, love and substance?

Joshua had helped Moses lead the Israelites out of Egypt. It had been a long and difficult journey – so long that the beloved Moses didn't see the end of it. Throughout their trek, the people had been the usual human assortment of cheerful, cranky, morose, loving, recalcitrant and courageous, but Joshua was troubled by their lack of commitment to the Lord, the One God of Israel. While enslaved in Egypt, some had worshipped the Egyptian deities. After arriving in Jericho, some had adopted the religious practices of the Amorite people they had conquered. Joshua was about fed up with their fickleness, so he gave them the message he had received from his highest understanding of God.

Which God will you serve, now that you have a deeper understanding of yourself as a spiritual being? Will you serve the God of your family of origin? Perhaps there are elements of that God that align with your highest understanding and other elements that do not. Will you serve the God of your neighbors or coworkers? You may find their God to be embracing and affirming.

Will you serve the God presented by Madison Avenue in print and television? Only as far as it aligns with your highest understanding of Truth!

Knowing yourself as a beloved child of God takes a lot of practice. The world surrounds us with evidence to the contrary! But every time we return to the Silence, reconnecting our consciousness with the infinite love and life of the creator of the universe, the truth of our beings resounds within us. Holding every thought, word and deed up to the light of your highest understanding of Truth requires constant diligence, constant discipline. It's exhausting – except that after you have a few triumphs, a few "course corrections," the exhilaration of knowing it <u>can</u> be done refuels and redoubles your efforts.

You <u>can</u> change your mind and change your life. You <u>can</u> dredge the cultural and societal sludge from your mind and heart, clearing the channels for divine love and wisdom to flow freely into your daily life. Just think – what if you never felt limited by anything, ever again? What if you believed in yourself so intensely that you could honestly say, "Of course I can!" to your heart's fondest and most secret desire? Beloved, choosing to serve the Lord of your Being, the highest intelligence and the deepest love in the Universe, will take you there. I wish for you a path of delight – and adventures of challenge. I wish for you the deep soul assurance that you are, right now, with no alterations or adjustments, the precious, beloved Child of God. I wish you your very own everyday spirituality!

With deepest love and richest blessings,

Brenda Strickland
March, 2015

Appendices

I.   **How to Journal**

II.   **How to Meditate**

III.   **How to Affirm**

I. *How to Journal*

The word "journal" is from the French word for day, *"jour."* It's daily writing. A journal can be an appointment book, or it can be a diary. In the case of this work, it's a vessel for thoughts and feelings expressed on paper either in words or sketches or both. It could include clippings, pressed flowers or other memorabilia, but the most important thing is that it includes the essence of each day.

Some people like to end the day by writing in their journals for a time before retiring for the night. Others prefer to start the day with writing to clear their heads. Writing can precede meditation time or follow it or both. Sometimes meditation yields important insights that belong in the journal, so it might be handy to have it available when meditating.

Please consider your journal your newest confidante. It can be the place where you pour out your heart or work through a challenge. A journal can be a record of a struggle or the story of a triumph. Sometimes life unfolds over weeks and days; keeping a journal can help you recapture the wonder of that unfoldment.

If you are facing a major change or stressor in your life, your journal is your best friend. By writing out your thoughts and feelings on a regular basis, you get them out of your head and onto paper where you can look at them more objectively. Sometimes the very process of writing out a worry brings the solution into focus where you couldn't see it before.

You may find yourself feeling uncomfortable with the idea of writing at first. If so, give yourself a specific task such as "I will write whatever comes into my head for 10 minutes – and that's all." Then sit down for 10 minutes, and if all you can think of to write is "I don't know what to write, but I have to sit here and write for ten minutes, so here I go writing for 10 minutes. Ten minutes is a long time, but I have to write that long so I might as well keep writing. Don't know what I'll write about, but they tell me it'll be good for me, so here I go. Writing for 10 minutes . . ." When faithfully practiced, this routine of emptying surface thoughts can open a deeper vein of Truth within you.

Another way to journal is to sit down and fill one page with things, people or events for which you are thankful. Or write an imaginary letter to someone, and tell them all about whatever is on your mind. Keeping a journal is a gift to yourself because it implies that you and your thoughts are worthy of being recorded. Give yourself that gift – just for the next six weeks – and see what blessings unfold!

II.   How to Meditate

Meditation is listening to God. It's not so much what you <u>do</u> as what you don't do. You may not actually <u>hear</u> anything – but eventually, if you practice enough and get quiet enough, you'll feel something deeply profound and vitally authentic. It'll be something that you may never have felt before, but it will feel as if you've known it forever. Learning to sit in the Silence, hold your mind in alignment with perfect stillness and "listen" for God's inaudible voice is the most powerful gift you can ever give to yourself and to the world.

One pundit gave very specific instructions for meditation, saying "Sit down and shut up." That's basically all there is to it – sit down, and stop all your physical, mental and emotional activity. Stop doing, and just <u>be</u>. Breathe in and out. Wait to see what your next thought will be, then let it go, and watch for the next one. Just keep letting the thoughts go by and waiting to see what the next one will be. What you may not notice is that the spaces between the thoughts will grow longer and quieter until you forget that you were waiting for a thought, and just rest in the Silence. That's meditation.

Some basic steps might include finding a place where you will be undisturbed and where you can be physically comfortable. Some schools of thought will suggest specific positions for the body; most agree that sitting with the back straight and eyes closed is important.

Some meditators like to stretch the body a bit before sitting – perhaps a little yoga to loosen up the muscles and joints. Some recommend reading or reciting a favorite prayer or poem to bring the mind into alignment with the Divine.

Breathing is an important element of meditation; many disciplines use rhythmic breathing to focus the mind and relax the body.

If meditation is new for you, try this sequence:

➢ Quiet your environment: close the door, dim the lights, silence the phone and request that others not disturb you.

➢ Sit comfortably, whether on a chair or on the floor, making sure your back is straight and supported as needed. Set a joyous intention of success and satisfaction as you settle in.

➢ Take a deep breath in, hold it briefly and then let it out. Feel any tension drain from your body as you exhale. Close your eyes and repeat as needed until your body is relaxed and mind is quiet.

➢ Bring your attention to a word or an image that means pure goodness, love or peace to you, and hold that word or image gently in your awareness. Allow your mind to revolve around that image, bringing the mind back gently if it strays away. Continue to breathe gently and hold that word or image, allowing it to fill your awareness, bringing the mind back into alignment with it, until you feel whole and complete.

➢ From your wholeness and completeness, before you emerge into your outer world, give thanks for the blessing of a time of quiet – no matter what your experience was. And then promise yourself that you'll do it again tomorrow.

➢ If you wish, write a few observations in your journal about your experience.

Beyond these basic introductory steps, you can access a universe of guided meditations on CDs, written meditations in books, formal instruction in meditation classes and your own experience guided by your own intuition.

You may have no idea how powerful your meditation consciousness is – or can be. Give it a try – the world awaits your amazing insights!

III. *How to Affirm*

An affirmation is a statement. Affirmations are used as tools in shaping consciousness, grooming one's mental habits for more pleasing results. An effective affirmation is one that easily and gracefully bridges the "is/ought gap" – the distance between what is and what we wish to be.

In order for an affirmation to be effective, it must slip easily into the normal flow of thought and feeling. If a statement feels untrue or false, the mind may not accept it, thus defeating the whole purpose.

When crafting an affirmation, start by taking your imagination to your desired destination – the feeling, vision, sound, taste and smell of your heart's desire. Name that destination with as few words as possible – a noun with only a few modifiers – and then build a statement that evokes the emotion of having arrived there.

An affirmation is not a goal statement – it doesn't need specific dates, times, amounts or details. An affirmation is a feeling statement, designed to remind you of the miracle you're approaching. It's almost as if you've returned to the present moment from the future, in which you've already experienced the attainment of the state you desire and you're just prepping yourself to go there very soon.

So, for example, Mary Morrissey in "Prosperity Plus" uses the lead-in phrase, "I'm so happy and grateful now that . . ." to slip that amazingly potent image into the mind past any objections from the "reality-based" part of the mind.

Maria Nemeth, in *Mastering Life's Energies*, acknowledges that sometimes we have a lot of compelling evidence lined up to prevent us from making important changes in our lives. She recommends using the phrase, "Nevertheless, I am willing to . . ." as a detour to circumvent thoughts of "I can't possibly do that because . . . !"

If there is a thought that stubbornly persists in trying to talk yourself out of your dream, you may wish to use a cleansing statement in the form of a denial. A denial is a statement that removes or negates the power or influence of a particular limiting thought. A denial might use the words "release" or "let go" or "no longer." It is short, sweet and to the point, like a verbal feather duster to sweep away the cobwebs of doubt, fear or failure. The word "nevertheless" acts like a denial in that it lifts your personal power above any perceived limitation.

Words like "try" or "hope" dilute the power of your affirmation. They water down the intensity of your intention because they shift the focus from the achievement of your dream to the effort of achieving it.

God is absolutely on your side in achieving your heart's desire, so including the name of God that resonates best with you is a good way to add some extra power to your affirmation. And because it is God in you that is doing the work, claiming that oneness will anchor your affirmation in your own relationship with the God of your highest understanding. You might also open your dream to divine intervention by adding "this or whatever is better in Your sight, Lord!"

Experiment with some of these phrases, as if you were building your affirmation out of Lego blocks:

94

I release _____.

I let go _____.

I no longer_____.

Nevertheless, I am willing to _____.

I rejoice and thank God that _____.

I praise and bless _____.

I'm so happy and grateful now that _____.

Once you've crafted an affirmation that makes your heart sing, put copies of it everywhere – the bathroom mirror, the refrigerator door, your wallet, the kitchen table, the dashboard of your car – and say it out loud as many times a day as possible. Make it into a song or a rap. Chant it as you work out, walk, ride your bike, vacuum the carpets. If it starts to lose energy, make up a new one that gets you going again. Imagine a beloved teacher, coach, friend, parent, aunt, uncle or grandparent saying it to you with great pride and love. And above all, remind yourself that your creator's will is always the highest and best for all concerned – including you!

About Brenda

Brenda Strickland is an author, educator and speaker. For several years she has been a dynamic and moving speaker committed to empowering people.

She is often asked to give workshops on Everyday Spirituality, in which participants discover their spiritual gifts and apply those gifts to their life's intentions. One participant commented, "In one hour, you helped me solve a problem I've struggled with for six months!"

Brenda has given her Voice Production Workshop for many organizations including the Honeywell Engineering Department in Puerto Rico. She says, "Your natural voice is more unique than your fingerprints. Your voice production is vital." A participant commented, "When you know the mechanics, you are empowered to speak and get your message across."

A gifted professional pianist and singer, Brenda holds Master's and Bachelor's degrees in Music Education from the University of Missouri at Kansas City. She taught elementary music classes for 35 years in schools from Kansas to Hawaii to Georgia, helping children find their musical voices as they celebrated the music of the world.

In recognition of her contributions to spiritual education. Brenda has been inducted into the Morehouse College Board of Sponsors.

Brenda and her husband, Rev. John A. V. Strickland, Senior Minister of Unity Atlanta, live in Dunwoody, Georgia. They share their home with their long-haired Dachshund, Duke, and their two cats, Makikilani and Bojangles.

www.ingramcontent.com/pod-product-compliance
Lightning Source LLC
Chambersburg PA
CBHW021410170526
45164CB00002B/585